WINTER HIKING and CAMPING

WINTER HIKING and CAMPING

by

John A. Danielsen

Third Edition

ADIRONDACK MOUNTAIN CLUB
GLENS FALLS, NEW YORK

Copyright © 1972, 1977 and 1982 by the Adirondack Mountain Club, Inc. All rights reserved. No portion of this material may be reproduced in any form by any process without permission in writing from the Adirondack Mountain Club, Inc., 172 Ridge Street, Glens Falls, N.Y. 12801. Printed in the U.S.A.

Library of Congress Cataloging in Publication Data

Danielsen, John A.
  Winter hiking and camping.

  Bibliography: p.
  Includes index.
  1. Snow camping—Equipment and supplies. 2. Hiking—Equipment and supplies. 3. Snow camping—Northeastern States. 4. Hiking—Northeastern States. I. Title.
  GV198.9.D36   1982   796.54   82-11456
  ISBN 0-935272-20-8

The most precious things of life are near at hand, without money and without price. Each of you has the whole wealth of the universe at your very door. All that I ever had, and still have, may be yours by stretching forth your hand and taking it.

—John Burroughs

CONTENTS

Page

FOREWORD vii

FIRST PRINCIPLES 1

THE BODY AND THE COLD 11

CLOTHING 27

EQUIPMENT 49

FOOD 109

TRAVEL 117

SHELTER 150

FINDING POSITION AND DIRECTIONS 159

SURVIVAL AND RESCUE 169

MOUNTAIN WEATHER 186

YOU AND THE ENVIRONMENT 200

APPENDIX 205
 Terrain Features—High Peaks of the
 Northeastern United States—Metric Equivalents
 —Books on Hiking, Climbing and Skiing,
 Western United States—Books and Articles on
 Natural History and Ecology—Bibliography and
 References

INDEX 217

PHOTO ACKNOWLEDGMENTS

ADK Search and Rescue Team
Adirondac
L.L. Bean Incorporated
Bob Cary
Almy Coggeshall
E. I. DuPont DeNemours & Company
Elkem-Spigerverket A/S
Eureka Tent Inc.
Exel-Silenta, Inc.
Fabiano Shoe Co.
Ferno Washington Inc.
C. Goetze
Leon Greenman
Trudy Healy
Carl E. Heilman II
Holubar Mountaineering Ltd.
Jansport
R. Johnston
Lowe Alpine Systems
Dr. William J. Mills, Jr.
Mountain Safety Research, Inc.
Museum of the American Indian
John Myhre
Frank J. Oliver
Optimus International
Precise Imports Corporation
Recreational Equipment, Inc.
Rivendell Mountain Works
Rustadstuen Pulkfabrikk
Sherpa Design Inc.
Silva Company
Clyde Smith
G. Milton Smith
The Snocraft Corporation
Staatsburg Tool Corporation
Times Mirror Magazines, Inc.
Union Carbide Corporation
U.S. Army Natick Development Center
U.S. Ski Association, Central Division
Jakob Vaage—Norway

FOREWORD

The goal of winter hiking and camping is to enjoy the winter scene and the outdoor experience to the fullest. To do this one must understand the preparations and precautions necessary in advance of a trip and during it. Winter excursions are not for people who ignore sound advice.

This book is introductory—it deals with the fundamentals. It is primarily concerned with conditions in the New York-New England area with its extensive forests and trail systems. It offers advice to make winter outings not only more enjoyable but safer, whether one is on a casual walk, a ski jaunt down an old woods road, or a backpack trip to the high peaks. Subjects are treated in a practical manual style as concisely and clearly as possible. Those seeking more detailed, technical information can refer to the publications listed in the Bibliography.

The book's scope is somewhat open-ended in that it contains some subjects, such as avalanches and avalanche school, snowhouse construction, and guidance from stars, that are not generally applicable to New York-New England conditions. Rock and ice climbing have been purposely omitted.

As a practical way of enhancing explanations, equipment is illustrated wherever possible. This has been done with the help and consent of the organizations cited. Such illustrations do not imply endorsement of any particular product.

Much in this book is owed to the generous advice given by many winter veterans: Almy D. Coggeshall, Robert L. Collin, Robert Gilchriest, Trudy Healy, Richard Jablonowski, Will Merritt, Gardner Perry III, Fay Welch, and Leon Barry. Acknowledgment of assistance is also due to Scandinavian Airlines for the snowhouse drawings from their Arctic Survival Guide; Eastman Kodak Company for data on cold-weather photography; the Appalachian Mountain Club and Jack Pangburn of ADK for help in obtaining photos; Leon Greenman for data on snowshoes; Bjorn Kellstrom for information on compasses; Union Carbide Corporation and Duracell International Inc. for temperature effects on dry cells; Raymond Chodkowski regarding operating an automobile in cold weather; and Dr. William J. Mills, Jr. of Anchorage, Alaska, for permission to use the frostbite photos. Thanks are due also to the many persons and organizations who contributed other photographs. Artwork was done mainly by Thomas Eaglin, Trudy Healy and Jane Bruner. Jack Drury and Tony Goodwin critically reviewed the third edition manuscript. Carmen Elliott of the ADK staff saw the book through production.

The fact that this book is in its third edition demonstrates to me that there is a continuing need for a good winter manual. I sincerely hope that the "project" will continue in the years ahead.

J.A.D.

First Principles

THE MEANING OF COLD

MOST ASPIRING winter hikers and campers come from well-heated homes, travel about in comfortable cars and trains, work in offices with a well-regulated atmosphere, and in general spend much time indoors during winter. Unless they are inveterate skiers, winter hikers, or part-time milkmen, they know little about the cold. To them cold perhaps suggests discomfort and ultimate flight to a heated shelter. It need not be so. There are many who have spent much of their lives outdoors in a cold winter climate, and who meet the challenge of the cold with deep enjoyment.

People differ substantially in their physical ability to tolerate cold. This ability is affected by physical condition, age, and race[33, 46]. Man's biological development has occurred in both temperate and tropical areas of the world; thus body functions and structures in some peoples have become adapted to regional climate. The natives of Tierra del Fuego and the high Himalayas could sleep outdoors with little or no covering. The Eskimo (Inuit) can put his hand into ice water and feel little or no discomfort.

Most people who are young and in good physical condition can tolerate the cold well. Persons exposed to cold for long periods can become more or less acclimatized. For short periods the evidence as to acclimatization is inconclusive, except as to hands and feet. But winter excursions involve much more. Before you start trailing up and down mountains on snowshoes or skis with a pack on your back, you must be ready. Successful — and safe — winter hiking and camping depend primarily on the full appreciation of winter problems and mental accommodation to them.

Let us understand:

First—the human body: Life can be maintained only by keeping the core of the body at a fairly constant temperature. Extremities are particularly vulnerable to frostbite. In the cold, food becomes more important as a source of energy and to maintain body heat—not merely to please our taste.

Second – travel and clothing: Snow and ice on the terrain involve several special problems. Travel is slower and more

2 FIRST PRINCIPLES

Winter hiking is fun!

It's minus 12 degrees in the Catskills.

difficult than in summer; fewer miles—or yards—are covered. Only about half as long a trip, on the average, can be successfully done in winter. Low temperatures require more and better insulating clothing, which is usually bulky and awkward, often making trivial tasks difficult and time-consuming. And clothing must be kept dry.

Third — the terrain: A snow-covered wilderness landscape tends to look unfamiliar. Many landmarks are buried, so that knowing where we are and where we are going depends on a far sharper and more constant use of mental faculties than in summer. Map, compass, and general familiarity with the area are absolutely necessary.

Fourth — the weather: Severe and varying weather can compound winter problems. Sudden thaws or rain should be anticipated. Warm weather can make snow stick to snowshoes in heavy chunks, as well as melt on clothing. Getting wet from melting snow or rain is a serious matter unless dry clothes and shelter are readily at hand. People have died of exposure even at temperatures well above freezing. High winds may force you to abandon your objective if it is an exposed peak or ridge.

LEADERSHIP AND ORGANIZATION

Day hikes are usually informal affairs—a party of friends, a club outing. The former may operate with or without a leader or leaders. Club outings have leaders, sometimes co-leaders. The more difficult the objective, the greater the need for leaders and leadership.

For safety, winter mountaineering trips should include at least four members. In the event of sickness or injury, one person would stay with the victim while two go for assistance. Two are needed for mutual security; each should have the physical strength to reach help. The party as a whole should be limited to a manageable number—in general, not more than eight in a group, including the leader. The actual limitation for a particular trip should be decided by the leader. For example, for a strenuous overnight climbing trip to the summit of a high mountain, the number may be restricted to the leader and four others. Exceeding a reasonable limitation can have results that may seriously affect the safety of the party, the environment in which the party travels, the ease with which the party functions during the trip, and ultimately how much enjoyment is achieved.

Too many persons make management and communications more difficult and time consuming. Greater time is expended in getting to the starting point, assembling gear, checking equipment, and getting set to leave. When individual and group problems are added to problems caused by harsh weather, the total effect can be compounded to an unacceptable level. A pack has to be adjusted; someone feels cold; a snowshoe strap breaks; eyeglasses get fogged; someone needs to put on sunglasses or drops a mitten.

A large group tends to spread out more on the trail. The tendency is for stronger hikers and the leader to keep going rather than to stop when necessary for the tail group to catch up. With a spread-out group, communications become more difficult or may be entirely absent. The risk of the group splitting up without the knowledge of the leader is much greater.

Having too many in a group has a greater impact on the environment. Human waste in a particular area is apt to be excessive and probably disposed of in unacceptable places. Vegetation in a camping area or off the trail, particularly on mountain summits with their sensitive and fragile alpine or near-alpine plants and soils, easily can be damaged by uncontrolled, herd-like travel.

Comparatively short hikes over easy terrain are often undertaken by a party of less than four. The decision to start a hike with less than four should be made with full knowledge of the possible consequences.

A hike leader should have the basic qualifications of physical endurance, familiarity with the local trail system, experience on previous winter trips, mature judgment, concern for others, motivation and courage, and ability to function in a stressful situation. Leadership means being responsible for safely guiding a group not only to the goal but back again.

The leader may have to decide whether he or she has sufficient confidence and ability to conduct the trip. In making decisions the leader can consult with other experienced members of the party, who are usually glad to offer advice. A discussion in a democratic spirit—perhaps as to which trail to take, or whether to turn back—leads, or should lead, to a wise

Signing the register on entering the trail.

decision. This is the way many trips are regularly and successfully conducted.

Well in advance of any winter trip the leader must inform all prospective members of the party as to (1) degree of difficulty of the trip, (2) physical qualifications demanded, (3) plans for meals, (4) required clothing and equipment, (5) transportation plans, and (6) meeting place and route for the trip.

Before the party starts, the leader must be sure that every member is physically able to make the trip at the pace necessary for the enjoyment and safety of all. Many a trip has been spoiled, and even made dangerous, by the presence of one person who could not keep up. At the start the leader should also check clothing and equipment—including snowshoes, skis, and bindings — to be sure they are in proper condition. No member should be permitted to start with improper or insufficient clothing or equipment. The leader should be able to make, either alone or with competent advice from others, an estimate of the weather likely to be encountered. After starting, the leader should try to keep the group together, setting a pace geared to the slowest member. Too slow a pace may allow the party to get chilled; too fast a pace may cause overheating.

The leader and leader's assistant, if any, should not bear more than a fair share of the physical strain of breaking trail through snow. Each member of the party should take his turn out in front. The effort should be divided, so that no one member becomes prematurely exhausted. The leader, especially, must maintain an energy reserve for any emergency.

A leader should be bold, but not too bold. If the weather is too severe, or the group lacks the physical ability to reach the top, or the climbing becomes so difficult that the party's safety is in doubt, the wise winter leader will sacrifice the objective. This must be done firmly, without recriminations. The real purpose in winter hiking and climbing is enjoyment, not needless risks. And that applies to everyone in the party. No one should be placed in jeopardy.

The above remarks apply to all hiking, climbing, and camping trips in winter. For extensive, difficult trips, perhaps involving weeks or months in mountains under severe conditions, special leadership and personal qualifications are of paramount importance.

Persons other than leaders also have responsibilities: (1) acceptance and acknowledgment of the leadership, (2) willingness to accept advice from the more experienced, (3) refusal to undertake a trip obviously beyond one's physical capabilities, (4) being prepared with proper and adequate clothing and equipment, and (5) remaining with the group from start to finish.

WINTER SCHOOLS

Winter schools around the country provide basic instruction, field experience, and leadership training in which one can participate to maximum advantage. Hiking clubs or their chapters may conduct short courses or lectures on winter subjects. Some colleges have courses in outdoor or environmental education which include winter instruction and field trips.

In the New York–New England area we have these winter schools:

ADK-AMC Winter Mountaineering School

A joint operation of the Adirondack Mountain Club, Glens Falls, New York, and the Appalachian Mountain Club, Boston, Massachusetts. There are three sections in the Adirondacks and White Mountains: *Beginner*—Day trips, workshops; *Intermediate*—Overnight camping (5 days), day trips, workshops; *Leadership*—For potential leaders and persons with previous winter experience; emphasizes group leadership, steep slope climbing, day and overnight trips.

Outward Bound (National office, Greenwich, Connecticut)

Hurricane Island, Rockland, Maine

Features 6–22 day courses in the White and Mahoosuc Mountains.

All five of the OB schools in the country offer winter courses. Other schools are in Colorado, North Carolina, Oregon, and Minnesota. Course content varies according to school location.

Standard courses in the instruction phase include physical conditioning, food planning and preparation, safety, search and rescue, first aid, ski touring, snowshoeing, navigation, snow shelter construction, expedition planning and control, cold injuries and treatment, clothing, and winter ecology. The trip phase includes a short expedition led by an OB leader, and a final expedition with minimum supervision, organized and led by students, of up to 4 days. Solo trips with minimum equipment of up to 3 days' duration may also be conducted. In the evaluation phase the experiences of the participants are recounted and discussed. OB emphasizes developing responsibilities to the group, teamwork, and individual initiative and resourcefulness.

The short course is a compressed version of the standard course.

There are also schools in Alaska and in the snow states of the Midwest and West. The two listed below may be of particular interest:

National Avalanche School (U.S. Forest Service, Fort Collins, Colorado)

Joint operation of the National Ski Patrol System and National Ski Area Association. A Phase I course of one-week duration is given in November of every other year in Reno, Nevada. Phase II consists of a group of "lab" sessions in February and March following Phase I at ski areas near concentrations of students who attended Phase I. Acceptance at the school is highly selective; attendance is tightly controlled. Students are selected from applications submitted in the early summer. A certificate of completion is awarded based upon satisfactory work and attendance. The USFS says, however, that possession of the certificate does not imply that a person is an avalanche expert. [*Note:* Avalanches are not generally as serious a problem in the Northeast as they are in the West.]

Boy Scouts of America—Okpik Winter Program

(National Cold Weather Camping Development Center, Ely, Minnesota (Moosehead Lake); and Northern Wisconsin National Canoe Base, Oshkosh, Wisconsin)

Weekend winter camping with instruction in basics of winter survival, equipment making, games, crafts, construction of snow shelters. The program is for boys 13 and over in supervised groups. Necessary winter clothing and equipment are furnished. Okpik is the Inuit name for the snowy owl.

REMINDERS

1. Never attempt an ambitious climb in a party of less than four members. Never climb without a leader equal to the possible emergencies.
2. Study a topographical map of the area before departure.
3. Have in the party a sleeping bag, a medical kit, and a hot drink in a vacuum bottle in the event of illness or injury. Emergency food also should be carried.
4. Be prepared with proper and adequate clothing for temperatures somewhat colder than are likely to be encountered. Frostbite is unlikely if the body is fully protected and certain recommended procedures are followed. Use a face mask when needed, especially on exposed summits.

ADK/AMC Winter School.

5. Plan to stay on known, marked trails unless you are an experienced winter hiker. Notify others of your route, farthest destination, and expected return time. Sign the register, if any, at the ranger station or trailhead.
6. Avoid overexertion. Don't participate in a trip beyond your physical capabilities. Know when to quit.
7. Keep all clothing as dry as possible. Brush off all snow. Control perspiration by slowing down your exertion, removing clothing, and ventilating.
8. Keep the group intact. Respect the leader's judgment.

The Body and the Cold

MAN'S CAPACITY to maintain a constant inner temperature gives him remarkable freedom to move about in various kinds of weather. Properly clothed, equipped, and fed, he can exist under extremes of tropical or polar conditions. The basic requirement is the production and regulation of body heat.

HEAT PRODUCTION AND CONSERVATION

Heat is produced in the body by chemical reactions, mainly oxidation of carbohydrates. Part of the heat comes directly from food, the body's energy source. Part comes directly from contraction of the skeletal muscles, involving consumption of energy stores.[6] Muscular contraction occurs either by voluntary exercise or by the alternating muscular contractions called "shivering." Shivering is fatiguing but helps to keep us warm. It diminishes with oxygen deficiency, breathing of carbon monoxide, or the taking of aspirin or alcohol. The body's ability to maintain warmth is depressed by lack of water, lack of food, fatigue, and shock—among other things.

Fig. 1 in a generalized way shows how the heat exchange takes place (refer to Table 1 for some percentage relationships). Most of our body heat is transported to the skin via the blood stream and tissues (convection and conduction respectively) and dissipated directly into surrounding air or clothing. Exposed skin is cooled by convection (any kind of air motion, including wind, across the surface), evaporation of perspiration, and by radiation — invisible infrared rays. Heat loss through clothing primarily involves conduction; some loss is caused by air movement and pumping action within clothing layers and by radiation. As the clothing absorbs perspiration, visible or invisible, from the body, or water from snow or rain, the clothing becomes more conductive. Loss is further increased by evaporation of moisture or ice at the clothing surface or internally, by the circulation of air at the clothing surface, and by radiation into space. Note that considerable heat is lost in breathing.

12 THE BODY AND THE COLD

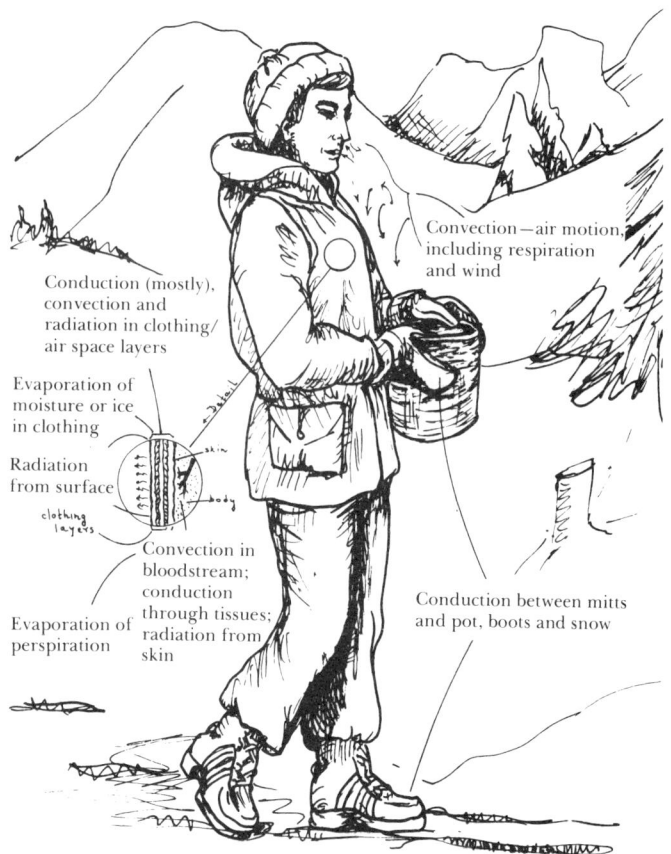

Fig. 1 —Heat losses by conduction, convection, radiation and evaporation (generalized).

TABLE 1
Ways in Which Body Heat is Lost[34]

Direct loss from body surface	63–70%
Evaporation of perspiration	14–18
Saturation of inspired (breathed-in) air with water vapor	8–9
Warming of inspired air (at −40°F)	2–9
Warming of ingested foods and fluids to body temperature	1 or less

When the skin cools, a reflex constriction of its blood vessels occurs, reducing heat loss. Thus, with respect to Fig. 1, one's internal heat is kept in balance by the body's automatic heat regulating functions, wearing adequate winter clothing, and taking other precautions.

When the internal body temperature drops below normal, shivering begins. The person feels chilly and develops "goose bumps." Teeth may chatter. Returning to a warm area or putting on additional warm clothing will warm the skin, and the chills may stop.

A cold weather phenomenon is the running nose. Air as it comes out of the lungs has been heated by the body and contains much moisture. Upon expiration, then, moisture condenses in the nostrils, accumulates there, and the excess runs out.

HYPOTHERMIA

A person who gets cold beyond the shivering stage is in serious trouble. Hypothermia, or subnormal body temperature, does not necessarily involve freezing of body tissues. Novice mountain climbers have perished from prolonged exposure to temperatures of around 50°F (10.1°C). Canoeists who have capsized in water at 40°F (4.5°C) have met a similar fate.

Any substantial cooling of the body below normal can be serious—perhaps lethal. Captain Hedblom in his "Polar Manual"[34] said: "Freezing to death in dry cold is a very pleasant way to go. Those who have come close describe the symptoms as extreme fatigue (only the *fatigued* sleep through the violent shivering), weak muscles, joint stiffness, and ultimately a feeling of warmth, comfort and an overpowering sleepiness. Unconsciousness and death follow painlessly."

To protect your own life and that of members of your party, anyone venturing on winter trails must know hypothermia symptoms and emergency treatment on the trail. Ignorance invites disaster. Inexperienced hikers without an experienced and competent leader are most susceptible. You may ask, "How is this possible?". Note carefully the events listed below. Cumulative effects of combinations of these events can result in a situation in which the risk of death from hypothermia is extremely high:

14 THE BODY AND THE COLD

Inexperience.

Ignorance about hypothermia — symptoms, emergency treatment.

Unfamiliarity with trails and area.

Absence of experienced and competent leader.

Number in party is less than four.

Party does not stay together; party does not stop when one member has difficulty keeping up.

No map or compass.

Lack of adequate sleep, rest and meals.

Lack of sleeping bag or insulated parka in party.

No hot drink or food in pack.

Choice of trip is beyond ability of party; trip route is not changed in accordance with ability of weakest member to complete original plan.

Victim is kept moving instead of being treated immediately.

Cap or mittens, or both, lost on trail.

Victim gets wet; dry clothes not put on; no spare clothing.

Improper clothing, such as cotton pants like blue jeans.

Bad weather—heavy snowfall, wind, rain.

Injury.

Exposed location of victim or party—ice and slope may prevent movement to a less exposed, safer position.

In the initial phase of hypothermia, the person is conscious of the cold, shivers intensely, and contorts his body in the effort to conserve body heat. When the body temperature falls below 92°F (33.6°C), the victim's face becomes pale and ghostly, eyes glassy, blood pressure and pulse rate depressed, mind confused. Errors of judgment occur. The body can no longer produce enough heat to maintain life. In this state *only the application of external heat can save the person.* If this is lacking, the body gives up the fight: blood returns to the skin, shivering and contortions stop, the sensation of warmth is felt. Death can occur at a body temperature of 75° to 78.2°F (25.8°C), although one boating accident survivor lived even though his temperature went down to 61°F!

Note below the hypothermic symptoms observable on the trail. Not all of these may be noticed. Other symptoms sometimes observed are muscle cramp, extreme ashen pallor, lightheadedness, and occasionally fainting.

SYMPTOMS

Unexpected and apparently abnormal behavior — often accompanied by complaints of coldness and tiredness:

Stumbling; awkward hand movements.
Unnoticed loss of cap or mittens.
Vision failure. It should be noted that vision failure is a very usual symptom. When it is noticed, the hiker's condition should be regarded with extreme seriousness.
Sluggish thinking and forgetfulness, including failure to respond to or understand questions and directions.
Some slurring of speech. Speech failure may not occur early; the victim may speak quite strongly until shortly before collapse.
Violent outbursts of unexpected energy, possibly physical resistance to help, violent language.

EMERGENCY TREATMENT ON THE TRAIL

1. Stop your hike; assemble all members of the party.
2. Get victim out of wind if possible.
3. Put on dry cap and mittens.
4. If backpacking and using a tent, put up tent—if feasible.
5. Put victim on foam pad or other insulation; remove boots, add dry socks; remove pants, shell parka and any wet layers underneath; put victim in sleeping bag or wrap the bag around him. Hikers usually don't carry a double bag, or two bags that can be zipped together, but if available, put victim and other hiker in it—both wearing minimum clothing.
6. If victim is slightly hypothermic, give a hot drink such as soup, broth, fruit juice, or chocolate, in small quantities (1–2 pints in an hour). If victim is severely hypothermic, do not give any hot beverage, as the benefit is slight and doing so may worsen the victim's condition. An alcoholic drink should *not* be given.
7. Do not allow victim to fall asleep.

Winter hikers have considerable exposure to low temperatures, yet the incidence of severe hypothermia and fatalities among them is extremely low. This is essentially due to the fact that hikers are usually adequately protected by clothing when

16 THE BODY AND THE COLD

A group nears the summit of Mt. Washington.

they start, are familiar with the trails and area, are well aware of travel limitations, travel in a cohesive group, and take other essential precautions. On the other hand, the incidence of deaths from hypothermia is much higher during other months of the year in high mountain country, such as the White Mountains. In the Whites, for example, people sometimes start hikes to peaks and ridges with summer or other light clothing, totally unprepared for the lower temperature and windy conditions, frequently accompanied by rain. Effective insulation of a wet hiker's clothing under these conditions can be essentially nil.

FROSTBITE

Nature of Frostbite

As a person becomes chilled, his body "thermostat" reduces skin circulation to maintain core temperature. This reduction introduces the hazard of frostbite.

THE BODY AND THE COLD   17

Frostbite is serious; it means pain and perhaps permanent injury. If rewarming is not done properly after deep frostbite, the loss of fingers or toes—even a foot or a hand—can result. Frostbite also means that other members of the party must end their trip prematurely in order to get the injured person to a hospital.

"Frostbite" is a general term applied either to actual freezing of tissues, with formation of ice crystals, or to reduced peripheral circulation, which may have results suggesting a deep sunburn. The less severe form of frostbite is called "frost-nip." Whether a person has frostbite or frost-nip may not be known for several days after exposure. Numbness of body parts, followed by tingling as they are rewarmed, is not true frostbite, which involves actual damage to tissue.

The body parts most susceptible are the nose, fingers, cheeks and chin, toes, and areas under pressure or wet, such as heels and feet generally. Frost-nip usually occurs in high wind or extreme cold, or both. Ordinarily, it is noticed as a sudden blanching or whiteness of the skin. If it is identified early and precautions are taken immediately, there is no tissue damage, and it can often be treated effectively by such means as a firm, steady pressure of a warm hand (no rubbing!). Chilled fingertips can be rewarmed in an armpit, or by putting them in the mouth. As warmth and color return, there is a tingling sensation.

Superficial frostbite usually involves skin and the superficial tissue just beneath it. The flesh appears white and waxy, is firm to the touch, but the tissue beneath is soft and resilient. When rewarmed, the injured area is at first numb, and mottled blue or purple; it will swell because of injured and leaking capillaries, and will sting and burn because of injured nerves. If damage is fairly severe and involves tissue beneath the outer layers of skin, there may be plasma seepage and resultant blistering. Throbbing, aching, and burning of injured parts may last for weeks. The area may remain permanently red, tender, and extremely sensitive when exposed to cold.

In deep frostbite, not only is the superficial tissue hard, white, and waxy, but the underlying tissue is hard, solid, and boardlike. The freezing involves deep tissues, including muscle and possibly even bone. The condition usually is accompanied by large blisters, which develop in three to seven days. The entire foot or hand will swell, turning blue, purple, or

18 THE BODY AND THE COLD

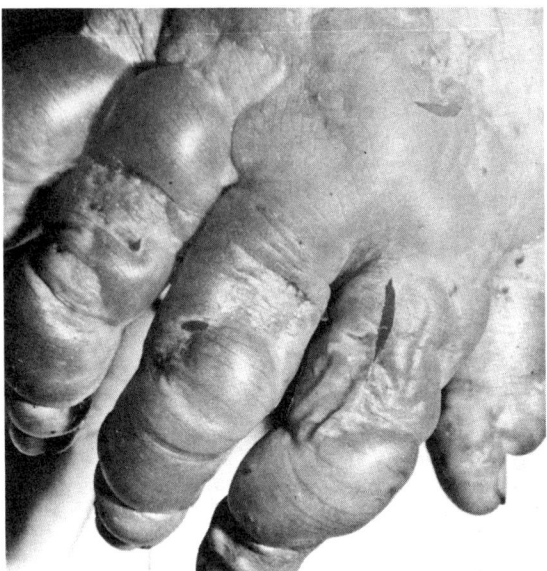

Fig. 2 — Serious case of deep frostbite. Photo taken seven days after injury. No permanent loss of tissue.

gray. After two days pains will be felt. This condition is very serious—a medical emergency.

Judgment as to whether frostbite is "superficial" or "deep" should be left to qualified medical personnel. On the trail, any frostbite other than "nip" should be considered as extreme.

Immediate Causes of Frostbite

Windchill on exposed skin: Our sensations of chilling effects of wind and temperature are mainly in our face and hands. Any skin that is not protected from wind is extremely vulnerable to frostbite. One must always be conscious of the chance of frostbite to the face under certain wind and temperature conditions since this is usually the only remaining unprotected part of the body. Studies of the effects of wind-chill on exposed flesh have been made by Siple and others, resulting in tables of

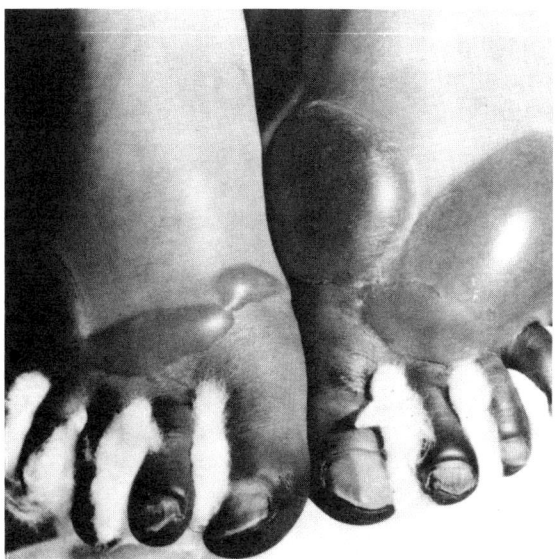

Fig. 3 —Serious case of deep frostbite, thawed with the old ice and snow method. All toes were eventually lost. Photo taken seven days after injury.

heat loss and so-called "wind-chill factors." However, such tables do not appear to be useful to winter hikers and probably frighten a lot of people unnecessarily. Furthermore, interpreting wind-chill factors to apply to portions of the body fully protected by clothing is not accurate.[29]

Frostbite of the face, particularly the cheeks, is easily avoided by getting out of the wind, turning one's back to the wind, putting on a face mask or cheek protectors, and extending and shaping the hood. When any of these steps are taken, the effects of wind and temperature are substantially reduced.

Effect of wind on the hands is obviously minimal as long as they are protected by a wind resistant mitten shell outside a warm mitten liner.

Heat loss of 1,400 Cal/m^2/hr has been calculated by Siple and Passel[58] to cause eventual freezing of exposed skin. Combinations of wind and temperature producing such loss were calculated as:

THE BODY AND THE COLD

Temperature °F	Wind Speed MPH
−40	2
−30	3
−20	5
−10	7
0	10
10	18
14	25
20	40

Rather than attempt to rely on any table on wind-chill factors, one may use this table as a guide. In other words, in addition to protecting other parts of your body by following directions explained in this book, be prepared to protect your face at modest temperatures and high winds as well as low temperatures and low wind speeds.

Wetting: As discussed elsewhere, cold air contains little moisture. Thus it tends to evaporate moisture from any wet surface, cooling it; wind increases the evaporation rate. In this way frostbite can occur. Feet in wet boots and socks, exposed to freezing temperatures, are susceptible because water reduces the insulating ability of the boots and socks. Gasoline or alcohol spilled on the hands or other body parts also can cause sudden chilling.

Exhaustion and fatigue: These reduce the body's ability to make heat directly from food or exercise, voluntary or involuntary.

Contact with cold objects: When bare skin—particularly if wet or damp—touches very cold metal, the skin instantly freezes to the metal. Serious tissue destruction occurs if the hand is jerked away. A pair of thin, dry gloves of cotton, silk, or rayon will prevent sticking, but since they provide little insulation frostbite can soon develop because of the high thermal conductivity of the metal.

Shock: This is a depressed state of body functioning that may be due to psychological factors such as fear, anxiety, or panic; or to physiological factors such as pain, massive loss of blood, or inadequate heart action; or to injury and massive tissue damage. Shock directly reduces circulation in the extremities, increasing the frostbite hazard.

Use of alcohol or tobacco: Alcohol dilates the peripheral blood vessels, thus increasing loss of body heat. Smoking constricts peripheral vessels, reducing circulation necessary to keep the skin warm.

First Aid for Frostbite

Only frost-nip can be treated on the trail.

Face: Place warm hand against face. Do not rub. Or place fur backing or mitten shell against the spot.

Fingertips: Put hand in warm armpit or under clothing, or use a hand-warmer if available. Put fingertips in mouth.

Toes (difficult to detect): Wiggle the toes to check whether there is any feeling. If not, remove boots, place foot on belly of trailmate*; cover with parka or shirt. After thawing, change to dry socks and dry insoles. Replace boots, lacing loosely to assure adequate circulation.

All other degrees of frostbite demand return to base camp or lodge as soon as possible; then the victim must be taken to the hospital. *Note:* Do not attempt to warm the frozen part until the victim is at a place where he can be kept warm continuously. Slow and inadequate rewarming on the trail, in a base camp or lodge, or anywhere else, followed by refreezing, can cause extensive tissue damage and later complications.

Rewarming of frozen feet on the trail turns the victim into a litter case, because his newly defrosted feet become tender and painful. It is better to walk out on frozen feet than to remain on the trail, although this may involve some warming of the feet during descent to a zone of warmer temperature.

Improper rewarming may result in further pain, death of tissue, and infection. Loss of toes or fingers, or at least a prolongation of recovery, may follow. Therefore, all attempts to rewarm should be postponed until the proper equipment and facilities for continuously maintaining controlled water temperature (100°F to 108°F—not exceeding the latter)[41] are available. In the New York–New England area these facilities would be found at a local hospital.

For further details consult an up-to-date manual on frostbite or take a course in mountaineering first aid.

---

*"This is believed to be the height of brotherly love and the hallmark of a true trailmate."—Captain E. E. Hedblom

Preventing Frostbite

Frostbite usually can be prevented by adequate clothing and experienced leadership with an understanding of weather conditions and the frostbite problem. The key to preventing frostbite is keeping body (core) temperature up.

Proper protection of the feet with appropriate socks and boots is mandatory. The boots must fit properly and not restrict circulation. Since socks when wet increase heat loss greatly, they must be kept dry if possible. A spare set should be taken along. Hands and face normally are protected from cold by adequate mittens and a face mask. Even so, it is important to conserve core heat so that blood circulation to the extremities is not reduced. Experienced mountaineers know that adding extra clothing to the trunk and putting on a hat will help to warm cold hands and feet.

To prevent frostbite, take these precautions:

Use proper clothing as outlined in this book.
Give up objective if the windspeed gets too high or other weather conditions worsen.
Eat adequate quantities of high-calorie, high-energy food, including ample fluids.
Avoid getting overheated (ventilate clothing, slow down rate of climb, control breathing).
Change socks, mitten liners, and boot insoles when necessary.
Avoid touching metal equipment with bare hands.
Avoid smoking or drinking alcoholic beverages.
Avoid spilling gasoline or alcohol on hands or mittens.
Avoid excessive fatigue.
Avoid constipation (it retards efficient metabolism).

Winter hikers who favor a beard should know that treatment of frostbite on a bearded face can be difficult. The beard may accumulate snow and ice, which prevents application of a warm hand to the skin. A beard may become solidly frozen to the parka, preventing removal of the garment until it has thawed. On the other hand, it has been reported that Eskimos at Wainwright, Alaska, develop the mustache to prevent the frost from forming on the upper lip and to protect exposed skin from wind-chill. If the eyelashes freeze together, do not try to pull them apart; warm with fingers.

Despite precautions, winter mountaineering does involve risk. The unpredictable may happen. According to Bradford

Washburn, frostbite "almost always seems to be related to other factors such as fatigue, sudden storm, an accident—or combinations of them."

DEHYDRATION

If the body is chilled, circulation through the capillaries is reduced. The heart must work harder—blood pressure and pulse rates go up. Urinary output increases.

Cold air has a powerful dehydrating effect. Air at −30°F contains much less moisture than air at moderate temperatures. Warming of cold air in the body greatly increases the ability of the air to hold moisture; thus this air tends to dehydrate the tissues. To this add the moisture loss from perspiration and elimination.

The result of all this is rapid dehydration unless ample fluids are ingested. While on the trail the winter hiker is unlikely to notice that he is becoming dehydrated. It is important, therefore, to drink lots of water and other fluids and not to delay this action intentionally. Fatigue, indigestion, and headaches may be the penalty. More than two quarts of water per day are needed for proper body functioning in the cold.

Sometimes excessive dehydration is caused by drinking too much of a stimulant. Caffein in coffee stimulates the nervous system, respiration, blood circulation, and intestinal and kidney functions, with resulting loss of body fluid. Tea and chocolate or cocoa are much less dehydrating than coffee.

SHELTER HAZARDS

If as little as 300 parts of carbon-monoxide gas (CO), one of the most lethal poisons known, per million parts of air is inhaled, it may cause a person to collapse. If air with 1,000 parts of the gas is inhaled for 3 hours, death will ensue.

Whenever a stove is used in a hut or tent for cooking and heat, carbon-monoxide poisoning is possible. Combustion of the fuel consumes oxygen, producing carbon dioxide mostly, also some carbon monoxide. Carbon monoxide is odorless, colorless, 97% the weight of air and accumulates in dangerous quantities if ventilation is inadequate. Because the gas is odorless, occupants of a tent or other closed shelter may be unaware of the grave danger.

THE BODY AND THE COLD

Symptoms of carbon monoxide poisoning: sudden headaches, weakness, nausea, sleepiness, perhaps heart palpitations. There is no single characteristic symptom, but the most noticeable clue is that the affected person breathes heavily when even slightly active.[45]

Be sure your tent or hut is adequately ventilated while a stove is in use. Don't fall asleep before taking proper precautions.

In tests made in a partially vented mountain tent of breathable nylon at the Worcester Polytechnic Institute,[40] it was demonstrated that CO is significantly reduced when the pot support is raised one inch so that the flame does not touch the pot. For the Optimus 111B stove, CO concentration declined from 98 ppm to a much safer 15 ppm; concentration from the Mountain Safety Research stove fell from 75 ppm to 18 ppm. It was concluded that incomplete combustion was caused by cooling of the flame by the cold pot. The report emphasized that the CO level also depended on stove performance, length of time stove is used, and tent ventilation.

Persons in a tight shelter such as a snowhouse can be affected by anoxia, or lack of oxygen, even in the absence of carbon monoxide. Minimal oxygen for survival must be available. In a candle-heated snowhouse, watch the candle flame; if it burns poorly or goes out, it is oxygen-starved. Open a vent low in the side of the shelter to get more air. A candle is a warning device as well as a source of heat and light. The size of a flame from a match or candle has been used as a practical indication of the lack of oxygen or the presence of carbon monoxide in a shelter. A match flame will go out when the oxygen content goes below about 15%[45].

Particular care must be taken with catalytic heaters, which may be used in a vehicle. Follow the manufacturer's instructions for the particular heater. At present there are no national safety standards. But these points should be noted:

- The gasoline or propane fuel in the heater burns at a much lower temperature—about 600 degrees lower than normal combustion—in the presence of a catalyst, usually platinum.
- After starting, combustion is taking place—using up oxygen.
- A flame is not visible.

Rather than risk death at night in a vehicle, which may be inadequately ventilated, it is best not to use the heater at all. Risk would be highest among inexperienced persons and ones who are unaware of the danger.

FIRST AID IN THE COLD

First aid in below-zero situations does not differ substantially from that recommended for warmer conditions. However, the cold has serious effects on an injured person, and practical, correct treatment methods must be thoroughly understood and employed. These effects and methods are emphasized here.

Treatment Methods

Shock: Even a minor injury can result in shock; so any injured person should be immediately treated for shock.

Loss of blood causes the arteries in the skin and muscles to constrict, thus shunting the available blood to the vital organs. This action is accompanied by an increase in pumping rate by the heart to maintain circulation and volume to the tissues. Shock results when this constriction and increased pumping are not sufficient to compensate for blood loss.

The heat-producing capability of the body may be lowered by injury, so that blood flow to the extremities and the skin is restricted to preserve the core heat. Thus the body's automatic responses from blood loss and reduced heat production hasten the onset of shock.

It is tremendously important, therefore, to immediately apply first aid for shock while efforts are made to stop bleeding and restore breathing. These measures should be taken:

1. Shelter victim from wind.
2. Put a down parka on victim and place victim in a sleeping bag or wrap the bag and other insulation around the person. Place maximum insulation, such as foam, underneath. Other hikers should lie or bundle next to him. Fill canteens with hot water and place in trunk area; use hot-water bottles when available.
3. Replace clothing if wet. Remove boots; examine feet; put on dry socks. Button up all clothing.
4. Give victim hot drinks and food when and if situation permits.
5. Consider whether victim should be lying flat or with feet elevated.

Bleeding: A tourniquet should be used only when all other measures to control bleeding fail. Its use involves serious risk of deep frostbite and possible loss of an extremity. A tourniquet may be put loosely in place and tightened only when necessary to stop uncontrolled bleeding. The cold will probably reduce bleeding and stop it sooner.

Fractures: Fixation splints (skis, ski poles, tent poles, or trimmed branches) should be used if the victim is more than an hour from a warm shelter. Splints should be well padded and tied snugly but not tightly.

First-Aid Kit

The kit for the winter hiker and climber is about the same as one recommended for other times of the year. Every hiker should keep a basic kit in his pack. Often he does not know the people who will be on his next winter outing, which may be an impromptu affair or a club trip. However, in a well-organized party not everyone needs to carry a kit. When checking equipment prior to starting, the leader should decide how many kits are needed. In addition to the basic kit, one person in a skiing party should have a 6-by-36-in. wire splint (made from ¼-in. wire screen). A pneumatic splint is definitely not advised for subfreezing temperatures, since the pressure necessary for immobilization increases risk of frostbite. An airlift would intensify the problem.[34]

Basic Kit

Broad adhesive tape or gauze roller bandage, or both
Bandaids (several sizes, and at least three of each)
Butterfly laceration dressings (at least three)
Sterile 3-by-3 in. or 4-by-4 in. gauze compresses (at least three)
4-by-4 in. compress bandage
Razor blade (single-edge)
Safety pins—several sizes
3 in. Ace elastic bandage
Small cake of soap
Needle and thread
Tweezers
Mole skin (for blisters)
Lip balm (small tube) (for chapped lips)
Aspirin
Salt tablets
Milk-of-Magnesia tablets (for indigestion)
Matches, "strike anywhere," waterproofed

Clothing

ABORIGINAL ESKIMOS (Inuit) managed to survive well for centuries in the Arctic with animal skins for clothing and an intimate knowledge of how to use them. They frequently wore only two clothing layers, totaling 12 to 18 lbs. Equal protection from woven fabrics and associated materials would weigh considerably more.

Winter hikers and climbers must use clothing intelligently, with full knowledge of how to get the most warmth and protection with the least weight.

BASIC REQUIREMENTS[9]

Insulating properties are of first importance. Insulation depends on the thickness of a fabric and the entrapment of still air within it. Such fabric should have low density and as much durability as possible.

Wool derives its insulating quality from the elastic, three-dimensional wavy crimp in the fiber that allows air entrapment in the spaces between fibers. Depending on the texture and thickness of a fabric, as much as 60–80% of wool cloth can be air. Wool can absorb plenty of moisture without imparting a damp feeling, because moisture "disappears" into the fibers. Under ordinary circumstances, moisture in a wool fabric may comprise 16–18% of its weight; maximum absorption can be as much as one third of its weight. Wool releases moisture slowly, with minimum chilling effect.

On the other hand, wool is relatively expensive and is uncomfortable when worn against the skin. Some people are allergic to it. It is difficult to repair and keep clean. During washing and dry cleaning, wool must not be violently agitated, otherwise felting may occur. Wool can shrink greatly unless specially treated. Moths thrive on it if the fabric is not mothproofed.

Cotton fabric has good qualities for winter clothing. Cotton (commonly used in parkas, underwear and inner socks) is inexpensive; it can be made strong and durable; it is easy to repair; it can withstand repeated washings and heavily soiled garments can be rubbed vigorously; it is pleasant to handle; it feels comfortable against the skin and does not irritate; and cotton fabric can be manufactured to effect considerable entrapped air (but less than wool) either internally or on the surface.

But cotton attracts and absorbs moisture. Under ordinary humidity conditions a cotton fabric may contain 6–8% moisture; at 100% humidity, 25–27%. Moisture can pass through cotton to be evaporated, but it dries slowly. And as a cotton fabric wears, it loses some of its fluffiness. It should be clearly understood that because of these moisture qualities, wet cotton garments have low insulating value. So, for a lengthy trip involving heavy energy expenditure or extreme or wet weather conditions, one should evaluate whether cotton garments like shirts, underwear and socks should be avoided.

Clothing items of nylon pile material—jackets, underwear, mittens, socks—now on the market raise the question of the relative merits of such material compared to wool. To cite one series of active and inactive climatic chamber tests where the test subjects wore equivalent wool and nylon pile garments in −20°C temperatures, the subjects in both instances felt warm and comfortable, and the measured variables, including the amount of accumulated sweat in the clothing, were not statistically different. The report[10] stated: "From a physiological standpoint there is no reason to expect artificial fibers to be inferior to wool in terms of providing insulation, as long as the thickness of the two types of garments is the same and the structure of the fibers and fabric is such that about equal amounts of air are trapped." With reference to preliminary experiments conducted by the laboratory and to the experiments mentioned above, the report concluded, "No significant differences could be detected between the two types of garments in terms of thermal insulation, nor in the ability to allow the free escape of sweat produced during physical activity. The present study confirms these findings."

To reduce the replacement of warm air by cold air in a fabric and to keep trapped air dry, a windproof and water-repellent outer "shell" is needed, consisting of a parka or anorak and wind pants. Lightweight clothing protected by a shell should form a system of layers. Insulation is enhanced by the spaces between layers. But the clothing must allow the body to be ventilated and rewarmed conveniently.

Be careful as to fit. Clothing should be loose-fitting to provide the necessary dead air space between layers and to allow adequate freedom of movement. A garment worn over others should be at least one size larger, but if it is too loose over them, there will be too much mixing of the air between and within layers as the clothing twists and shifts. Don't wear so many socks that the toes can't move freely.

The complete clothing assembly is necessarily bulky. If a garment happens to look neat or stylish, fine—but protection should not be sacrificed for appearance.

Clothing must be ventilated to allow moisture-laden warm air to escape and to minimize absorption of moisture. Outer clothing may accumulate well over half of the sweat produced, whether one is inactive or doing heavy exercise. With adequate ventilation—preferably to the point, initially, where one feels slightly chilled—exertion will not cause overheating, and the peeling off of garments can be kept to a minimum.

For ventilation (and buttoning up), clothes should include:

1. Loose-fitting parka with full-length zipper, with heavy plastic chain and metal slide, front closure, a waist tie, and wrist strap or Velcro ties, or knit cuffs. Large pockets may be installed inside the parka front for canteen and nibble food.
2. Shirt or quilted jacket, or combination, that can be opened completely down the front.
3. Mittens with strap or Velcro tie on the gauntlet, or elastic wristlets.
4. Pants held up by suspenders rather than a belt. If the pants have an adjustable waist tie or can be otherwise loosened, they can be ventilated. A belt around the waist would prevent ventilation, thus speeding up absorption of moisture. Unzipping the fly will definitely increase ventilation.

The need for loose-fitting clothing is complicated by the need to carry a pack. The carrying harness, hip belt and pack press the layers against the body, reducing their insulation value, impeding ventilation at points of pressure, and trapping moisture. Ventilation is improved by using some type of pack with a frame.

No clothing combination has yet been developed that will completely protect an inactive person for a long period in extreme cold. This means that if a person becomes inactive under winter conditions because of injury, exhaustion, weather, or otherwise, he will eventually become chilled. Some means—food, shelter, additional clothing, etc.—must be employed to arrest the loss of body heat.

Clothing assemblies suggested here are designed for a person who is active. Additional protection, such as a down parka, jacket, or vest, is advisable for periods of relative inactivity, such as lunch stops and camping. Clothing that could maintain body heat balance for many hours in extreme cold would be so bulky and heavy as to be entirely impractical.

TYPES OF CLOTHING

Underwear

Unlike the Eskimos, we of more temperate lands consider insulating underwear essential.

Choices of winter underwear are considerable, with many brands and fabrics on the market, including natural-synthetic blends and 100% synthetics. Considering the broad range of winter activities, environmental conditions, and individual factors, relative insulating and other properties of underwear cannot be simply compared. To do this, specific garments must be tested and evaluated in carefully controlled and managed tests. Under ordinary circumstances, the individual user is, or should be, the best judge of underwear to use after taking into account all trip and personal factors, including cost. Unless trip conditions are extreme, it seems appropriate to emphasize the outer clothing layers rather than underwear. One should avoid using too heavy underwear for less extreme situations as perspiration can be excessive and ventilation, especially for drawers, is limited. Finally, regarding relative thermal properties, one should remember that insulating value depends upon air trapped within a fabric and the fabric's thickness.

Fishnet — all cotton, cotton-synthetic mixture, or wool-synthetic blend—has very good insulating qualities, is relatively nonabsorbent, and is easy to dry. When wet, it is light. A well-fitting conventional knit undershirt may be worn over the net to make tight air cells. Whether this should be done depends on the relative importance at the time of insulation versus ventilation. Fishnet has good ventilating properties, so

CLOTHING 31

that a loose-fitting, full-opening shirt over it would be appropriate. One may also opt to use fishnet with vertical channels. (See Fig. 4.) If the rough feeling of the net against the skin is unpleasant, particularly when carrying a pack, consider using a net shirt with fabric shoulders or wearing a cotton-synthetic T-shirt underneath.

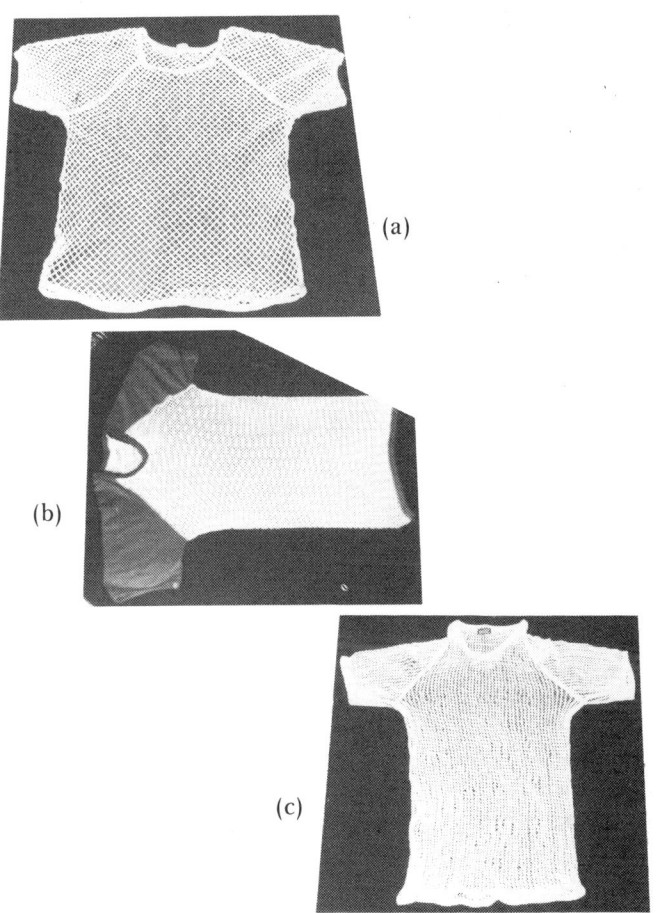

Fig. 4 — Types of string undershirts: (a) Uniform, all mesh; (b) Hiker's, with cloth shoulders and sleeves; (c) Vertical channel

Thermal knit—such as cotton-synthetic mixtures, or 100% synthetic—is a fabric with waffle-like impressions on the surface. Some prefer it to net because of skin comfort and feel. The surface impressions and internal trapped air provide high insulation value.

Conventional knit—100% wool, 50% wool-50% cotton inner layer, cotton synthetic mixtures, or 100% synthetic such as polypropylene, Vinyon-Acrylic—can contain lots of trapped air, depending on make. Lightweight types are generally not as good as fishnet and thermal knit, but are still useful for mild weather and short trips. To solve the irritation problem caused by wearing wool next to the skin, one can compromise by wearing a conventional knit with cotton as the first layer. Acceptance of cotton would allow better absorption, improve durability and feel, and improve washability.

Research reports indicate that close-fitting underwear replaces the boundary insulating layer of still air next to the skin, so that there is no gain in insulation, particularly in wind. Unlike tight-fitting underwear, then, it seems appropriate to choose loose-fitting pajama type underwear, such as the U.S. Army's, to get additional insulation from such boundary layer and other still air between the fabric and the body. An oversize 50% wool and 50% cotton conventional knit, with sleeves and legs cut, would do the trick.

In mild weather and when around a lodge, one can dispense with long drawers altogether. Wearing them indoors can be uncomfortable, and changing is a nuisance. A neat solution is to wear wind pants over your wool pants.

Shirts

Long, all-wool, tightly woven shirts of good quality, with squared-off bottoms, are recommended. A person who is allergic to wool can use shirts of various wool mixtures. For better ventilation, wear the shirt bottoms outside the pants.

Bodywear

The windproof shell over the trunk and head is essential to conserve body heat and to give some protection against rain and snow. The shell, preferably with a full-length zipper, should be large enough to cover all other clothing, including a reserve jacket or sweater, and yet allow maximum freedom of movement. It should cover the hips. It should have ties at the waist to stop ventilation and to create dead air space. For improved ventilation through the sleeves it should have adjustable straps or Velcro at the wrists, although some prefer knitted cuffs or elastic wristlets, particularly to prevent snow penetration. For carrying trail lunch, camera, cap, mittens, or other small items, the shell should have roomy pockets covered by flaps.

The hood should give maximum protection to head and face. Hoods for arctic parkas are made with a tunnel-like front supported by a wire that can be shaped. To prevent frost accumulation, the ruff would be trimmed with fur. Such a hood protects against winds from all directions except headwinds, but limits visibility and may impair one's ability to climb and descend.

The parka zipper should be a heavy-duty type. Now and then lubricate it with graphite or candle wax. The pull should have a thong or tape extension so that it can be pulled with a mitten.

Parkas are usually made of close-woven cotton-synthetic fiber fabrics of high strength and durability and treated to make them water repellent. The pullover type of shell, commonly called "anorak," used extensively for skiing may be of 100% nylon for strength and low weight.

When a garment has to be taken off, remove an inner one rather than the shell. Items that must be handy are left in exterior pockets (food, map, compass, camera, etc.). The shell protects a wool shirt or other layers from snow and resulting moisture. Removal and replacement of inner garments are inconveniences that have to be tolerated. When climbing strenuously in windless and sunny areas, one can hike with all top garments removed except the undershirt.

The garment favored for use under the shell has long been the wool sweater. Frozen moisture can be beaten out of it. But snow clings to it and it is not easily ventilated, unless it's a cardigan.

Today one can use the quilted jacket (with batts of Dacron, Orlon, or other materials). It weighs less than wool, has less bulk, can be fitted loosely, and can have a full zipper for better ventilation. The quilted jacket allows much body moisture to pass through the batts rather than accumulate. But if this jacket gets wet on the trail, you are in trouble. Its insulation value becomes practically nil, and adjoining layers of clothing are dampened. If the batts of a quilted jacket are secured with sewed-through seams, the insulation along the seams is negligible, just as in inexpensive sleeping bags.

A down jacket or vest provides more insulation, is lighter, and is capable of being compressed into a small bag, but is more expensive and loses much insulation value if wet. Jackets insulated with polyester filament, if wet, provide greater insulation.

New Fabrics

New materials in the form of waterproof, breathable fabrics such as Gore-Tex and Bukflex II have been developed in recent years. These fabrics allow body moisture vapor to escape through microscopic holes in a plastic coating or layer, yet prevent rain or other water from penetrating inward. The principal items of winter application are parkas and mitten shells. Gore-Tex is the trade name for a sandwich of thin, sponge-like plastic film (polytetrafluoroethylene, 0.001 inch thick—82% holes, 18% solid—nine billion holes to the square inch) between two layers of nylon fabric.

Although rain is encountered in winter travel, one usually does not have to be especially prepared for the event by having a parka of this new material. Items made of it would of course have utility in other seasons when hikers and campers have to deal constantly with the persistent rain-body moisture problem. The new material is relatively expensive, and the question is whether the additional cost is worth the advantage gained. Additional effort has to be expended from time to time in cleaning the fabric with alcohol or a water and soap solution, since the pores will eventually become clogged from oils from perspiration and wool or soiling from external sources. The seams tend to leak unless they are coated with the seam sealer supplied or are electronically sealed.

Pants

Closely woven, good-quality wool pants with flaps over the hip pockets and without cuffs (which catch snow) do nicely for snowshoeing and skiing. Roominess is needed for stretching and warmth. Adjustable waist tabs, or waist cord, and suspenders (fastened to loops or buttons) will allow you to ventilate.

The fashionable tight-fitting pants—especially blue jeans and the like—are not appropriate. For ski touring a pair of wool knickers gives you somewhat more freedom of movement around the legs in comparison to pants.

For extra warmth when stationary, use down pants over other layers. If you expect to be in considerable contact with snow, or you need wind protection, put on a pair of wind pants over your wool pants. Wind pants are easily pulled over the latter and hung from suspenders or secured to the waist with a drawcord. The leg bottom is secured outside the boot tops with drawcords.

Fig. 5 shows the scissors suspender, a U.S. Army winter issue not commercially available except as a scarce surplus item. One can make the suspender at home without too much difficulty out of 1½ inch elastic, 1½ inch webbing, and heavy wire. Unlike the conventional suspender, the Army suspender, with its two hooks, supports the pants (and long drawers or wind pants) from loops at the sides of the pants. It is not necessary to remove top garments when removing or pushing down the pants.

Gloves and Mittens

Maximum protection for the hands is furnished by mittens, not gloves. Mittens have less surface area through which heat can be lost. With a mitten however, manipulation is limited. The maximum practical thickness of glove fabric is about ¼ in., while that of a mitten is as much as 1½ in.

The mitten should consist of a nylon shell without leather palm, or a cotton shell with leather palm, a gauntlet extending over the sleeve cuffs, an adjusting strap (or Velcro or elastic wristlets) and a suspension loop, and wool mitten inserts to fit. For intense cold an insulated mitten insert can be used in place of the wool mitten. The back of some shells is covered with alpaca, which can be held against the cheeks to treat a nip. A new and useful mitten is one made of waterproof material over flexible, open-cell foam. For wet conditions this waterproof property is an advantage.

A point to note about wristlets: because they absorb moisture, they can eventually freeze, cause discomfort and lose their intended effectiveness.

36 CLOTHING

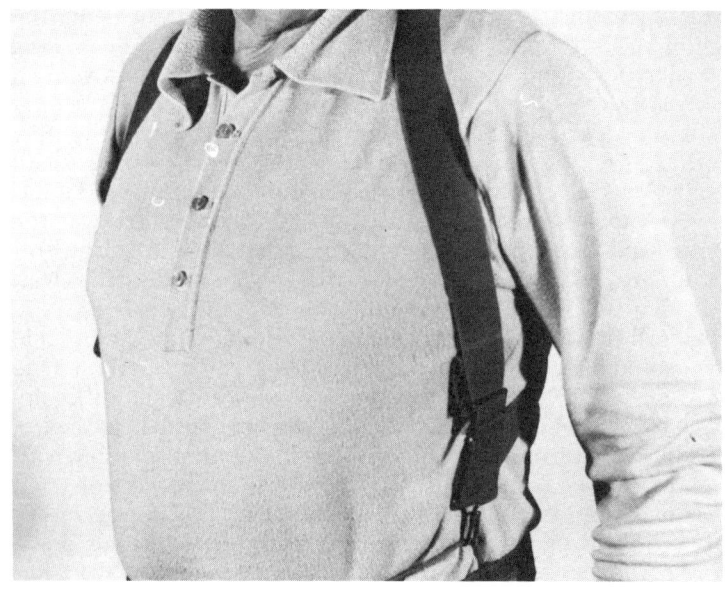

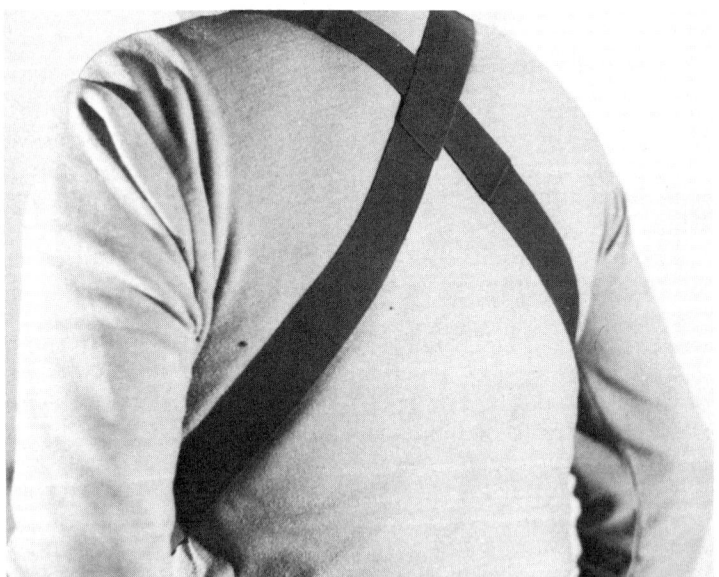

Fig. 5 — Scissors suspenders.

Mittens can be dropped and lost in the snow. Hands groping for dropped mittens in deep, powdery snow can get frostbitten. Mittens should therefore be fastened by a cord to the suspension loops on the gauntlet and secured around the neck. Alternatively, install D-rings in armpits of parka. Short mitten cords with snap hooks would be secured to these rings. This method prevents snagging on going through brush.

Even with this precaution, to be without a reserve pair of mittens or gloves could be a serious oversight. Mittens can get wet. Hikers should not depend on their buddies for spares. An extra pair of gloves, or mitten inserts at least, should be carried by each member of the party. In an emergency, extra wool socks can be used as mittens.

When manual dexterity is needed, glove inserts of wool, silk, or nylon can be worn. The complete mitten assembly or just the wool mitten insert will permit only the gross handling of objects.

How does one manipulate objects in the cold—instruments, stove, camera? It can be done if a person has been highly active just before, so that there is plenty of warm blood moving into the extremities. If practicable, use the wool-glove mitten insert, gun gloves with leather palms, fur-lined leather gloves with thumb and index finger slit, appropriate slits cut in thumb and palm of mitten insert for the thumb and index finger, or silk or nylon gloves. (The latter two are suitable where fine handling is needed.) Before the hands start to chill, put them back into the mitten shell, in the pockets, or under the armpits. Use a hand-warmer if available. One can also do simple exercises to increase circulation: clench and unclench the fist in the mitts; swing the arms, but as low as possible.

Once the hands have become chilled, it takes a long time to rewarm them.

Reminders:

1. If hands become too warm, remove inserts before hands start to sweat. Wear the shell only. Remove the shell, too, if necessary.
2. Put on reserve mittens immediately if regular ones get wet. When camping overnight, damp inserts can be hung to dry on a line in a heated tent. Damp inserts can be dried in one's sleeping bag during the night.
3. Keep mittens and gloves clean, as dirty pairs are less warm.

Boots

A satisfactory all-purpose boot for winter hiking, camping, snowshoeing, ski mountaineering, and kindred activities has not yet been developed. Nor has any boot been designed that will prevent heat loss while the wearer is inactive for a long time. Perhaps the best so far is the all-rubber, insulated boot introduced in 1951 by the U.S. Armed Forces to replace the shoepac and the mukluk.

The ideal boot should protect both the active and the static foot, in wet conditions as well as dry. So when we discuss boots, we must be aware of their limitations and of the need—not always recognized—for keeping the feet warm by exercise, by proper and adequate clothing about the trunk and head, and by eating high-calorie foods.

The choice of boots will depend on whether one will be using skis, snowshoes, or crampons or just hiking "barefoot." Kinds of boots, some of which are illustrated, are described in Table 2.

Now that boots have been chosen, how can snow be kept out of them? On a day hike on a packed trail you may not have a problem. If the snow is new and deep, or if you should get off the trail, you should be so dressed that the snow will not get into the boots and wet the socks. Snowproofing can be done by (1) installing a drawstring in the cuffs of your pants and fastening them outside the tops of the boots, (2) wearing shell pants with drawstrings in the cuffs over pants, or (3) wearing gaiters or overboots. Pants with drawstring cuffs can be used with ankle-high and higher boots, but for the former make sure the pants are long enough.

Fig. 6 — Military, all-black, insulated boot.

CLOTHING

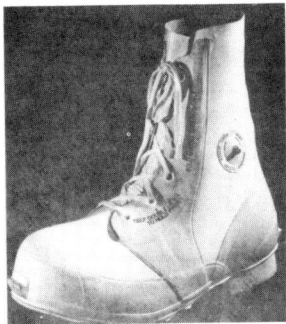

Fig. 7 — Military, all-white, insulated boot.

Fig. 8 — Insulated, leather-top, rubber bottom boot.

Fig. 9 — Felt insulated, leather top, rubber bottom boot.

Fig. 10 — Uninsulated, leather-top, rubber bottom boot.

40 CLOTHING

Fig. 11 —Leather mountaineering boot with insulating booties.

Canvas Mukluks

These can be made at home out of heavy canvas and leather. Fig. 12 shows pattern guides. Copy these patterns onto cheap material with some stiffness. Assemble these rough patterns with pins and adjust to size to make your own patterns, allowing for at least two pairs of heavy wool socks, felt insole, and extra material. Then cut the canvas from your personal patterns. The canvas sole should be reinforced by a leather sole (not shown) sewed to the former. A tunnel has to be made in the top of the upper for the drawstring. Sew or rivet loops to the front of the upper for the lashing tape that further secures the boot to the leg. Refer also to Fig. 16 as a guide.

For a different pattern see Edna Wilder's book on the Secrets of Eskimo Skin Sewing.[67]

Reminders:

1. Keep boots dry. Generally, a wet boot invites frostbite. (However, wearers of all-rubber or rubber-bottom boots

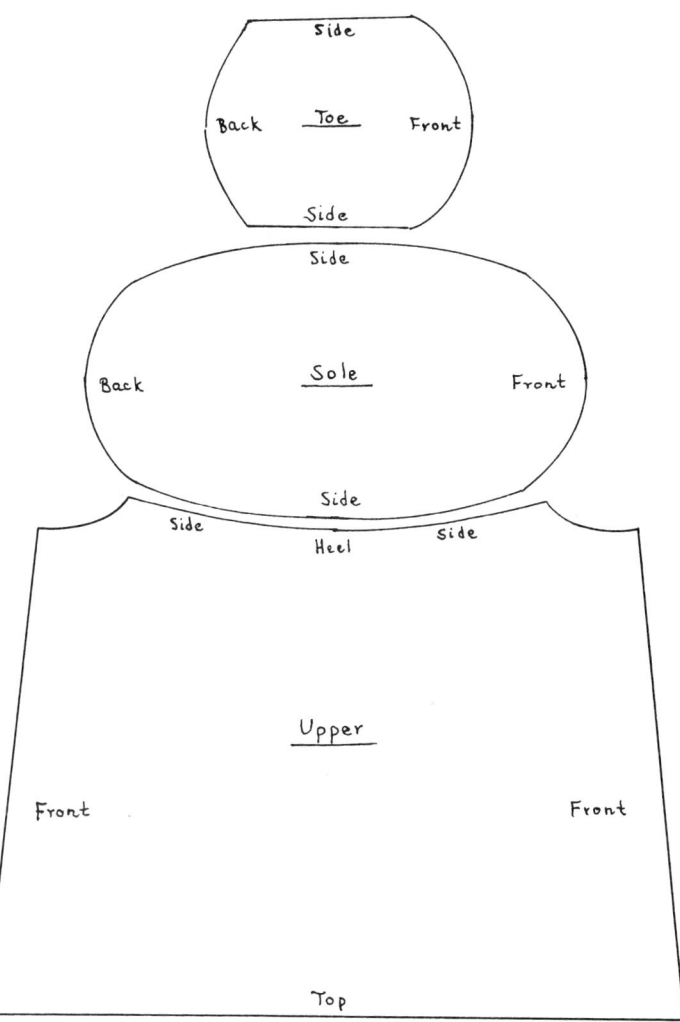

Fig. 12 — Pattern for canvas mukluks.

TABLE 2
Boots

Type	Description	Climate*	Sock, etc.	Comment
Shoepac	Rubber bottoms, leather uppers	Wet-cold	2 pairs: 1 light, 1 heavy. Substitute light wool with cotton-synthetic if wool-sensitive. Wear insole.	Hiking, snowshoeing. Feet will perspire because of rubber bottoms. Change socks when inactive. Can be worn with crampons, but refer to text. Should have lug sole for maximum traction. On descent with snowshoes, bottoms do not have adequate rigidity to prevent strain on foot.
Mukluk	Leather or rubber sole, canvas upper	Dry-cold	2 pairs (minimum) heavy wool socks or layers of duffle; felt insoles.	Can be purchased, or make your own. Fine as a change pair in camp. Cannot be used with skis or crampons, but suitable for snowshoes. Not waterproof—must be kept dry.
All-rubber, insulated (military)	Black, 11½" high, wool-felt insulation, all-rubber cleated sole, weight 5 lb, 8 oz., ski shelf on heel	Wet-cold	50% wool, 50% cotton, cushion sole. 1 pair only.	Designed for use in wet cold—not below −20°F. Change socks when wet. Wash interior of boots with soapy water. Be careful not to puncture boot. If punctured, insulation will get wet. Repair with rubber patch. May be used with snowshoes and crampons. Not rigid enough for extreme technical cramponing.
All-rubber, insulated (military)	White, 11¾" high, all-rubber, wool-felt insulation, cleated sole, weight 5 lb, 9.75 ozs., ski shelf on heel	Dry-cold	50% wool, 50% cotton, cushion sole. 1 pair only.	Change socks when wet. Wash interior of boots with soapy water. Be careful not to puncture boot. If punctured, insulation will get wet. Repair with rubber patch. Plug air-release valve. May be used with snowshoes. Has more insulation than black boots. Designed for −65°F; may be used at −80°F if active. Available but expensive—about $100 per pair.

CLOTHING 43

Type	Construction	Classification	Socks	Comments
All-rubber, insulated (commercial)	Foam insulation, wool felt insole with or without cleated sole	Wet-cold	2 pairs of wool socks	Inexpensive alternative to military boots. Not as good, but usually adequate for New York-New England conditions.
Mountaineering	Leather, insulated or uninsulated, with lug sole	Dry-cold	2 pairs of socks—1 light wool, 1 heavy wool. Insole	May be used with snowshoes and crampons. Fit must not be too tight with 2 pairs of socks and insole. Leather boots provide relatively little insulation. If inactive, feet will get cold.
Ski mountaineering	Leather, uninsulated, with lug sole, box-like toe.	Dry-cold	2 pairs of socks	Controlled skiing on steep slopes, narrow trails. May be used with or without crampons. Poor insulation. Consider using exterior insulation.
Ski touring	Leather, uninsulated, smooth sole	Dry-cold	2 pairs of socks	Cold unless constantly moving. Insulated boot for moderate cold available.
Felt	Rigid shape, all felt	Dry-cold	1 pair of heavy wool socks, or 1 thin and 1 heavy pair.	Excellent for camping; extremely light—0.75# per boot compared to 2# for uninsulated Bean boot. Not a hiking boot.
Overboot with insulated bootie	Insulated bootie and nylon outer boot with soft sole	Dry-cold	1 pair of medium weight socks	For camping and change of boots after hiking. Not a hiking boot.

*U. S. Armed Forces classifications:
Wet-cold: Where temperature changes rapidly in 14°–68°F range and rain, snow, slush, and mud would be encountered.
Dry-cold: For temperatures 14°F and below, and for extra protection against frostbite.

44 CLOTHING

quickly get wet feet from perspiration. An active hiker will have wet but warm feet.)
2. Change socks as often as practicable.
3. If the feet get cold while inactive, exercise the entire body. Put on more clothing.
4. If wearing all-rubber insulated boots, do not kick sharp objects. If the exterior is cut, the value of the insulation will be lost. Repair any punctures as soon as possible.
5. Talcum powder inside rubber boots facilitates getting them on.

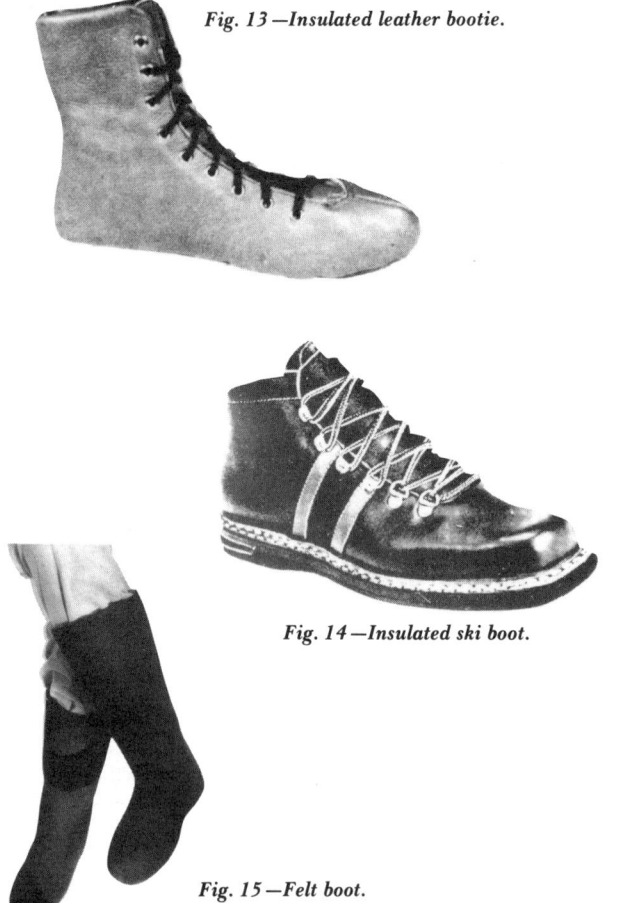

Fig. 13—Insulated leather bootie.

Fig. 14—Insulated ski boot.

Fig. 15—Felt boot.

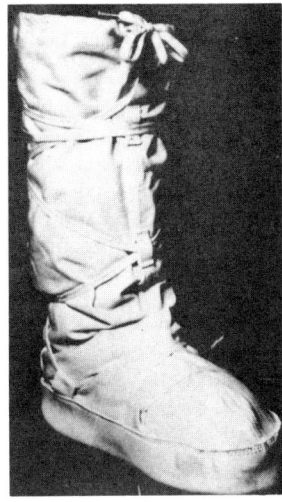

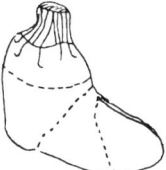

Fig. 17—Insulated bootie and overboot.

Fig. 16—Canvas mukluk with leather sole.

Creepers

Fig. 18 shows two types of spiked devices for attachment to boots when crossing ice or hiking "barefoot" on frozen ground. *They are not substitutes for crampons.*

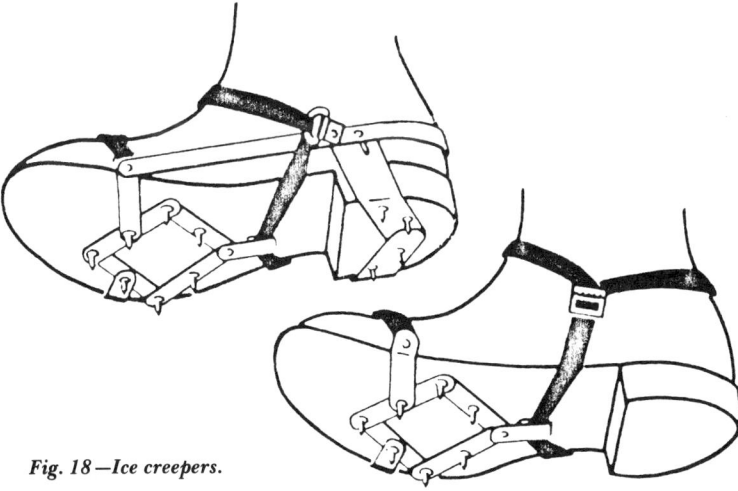

Fig. 18—Ice creepers.

Headgear

The head needs protection, because heat loss from the head is relatively rapid. Nose, cheeks, and ears are especially vulnerable to frostbite. Protection against wind can be provided by the parka hood. For warmth use separate headgear — any of the following:

1. Wool cap, plus parka hood (with or without tunnel)
2. Balaclava helmet plus parka hood (with or without tunnel)
3. Pile-lined helmet or down-insulated helmet

For extreme cold and wind it is important that the wool cap be extensible, so it will cover neck and face, except for eyes and nose. This cannot be done with the wool cap, which could be adequate for less extreme conditions.

The balaclava helmet is made of thick wool, is less wind-porous than the wool cap, and can be pulled down over the neck. It is commonly used in polar regions.

The pile-lined helmet is essentially a wind-resistant shell of durable material lined with alpaca pile or fur. It has ear flaps, which can be pulled down and secured with tape under the chin, and a visor that can be flipped up for better visibility. Unlike the balaclava helmet, it does not protect the neck completely.

Essential where strong, low-temperature winds are expected is a suitable face mask made of wool faced with leather or chamois. A nose and cheek protector may be adequate for less severe conditions.

CLOTHING CHECKLIST

Headgear

Wool cap
Balaclava helmet
Pile-lined helmet
Face mask
Nose and cheek protector
Hood with tunnel

Bodywear

Underwear
Wool, or other fiber, shirt

CLOTHING 47

Prepared for the cold.

Wool sweater or fiber pile jacket
Insulated jacket or vest
Parka (shell); anorak
Wool pants; knickers
Shell pants
Down, or polyester filament, parka—in stuff bag

Gloves and Mittens

Mitten shells with wool mitten inserts
Gloves—for dexterity
Silk or nylon gloves—for fine manipulation
Spare wool mitten inserts
Down, or polyester filament, mittens

Footwear

Ski touring boots
Ski mountaineering boots, uninsulated, with lug soles
Hiking boots, uninsulated, with lug soles
Hiking boots, with inner boots and lug soles
Rubber bottom—leather top boots
All-rubber boots, insulated, military, white
All-rubber boots, insulated, military, black
All-rubber boots, insulated, commercial
Mukluks
Felt boots
Overboots
Gaiters; touring boot socks, booties
Socks, felt liners, insoles

Equipment

PACKS AND FRAMEPACKS

FOR PACK AND FRAMEPACK details and evaluations, consult "Backpacking Equipment: A Consumer's Guide."[7]

Winter hikers and skiers should note pack features which facilitate operating in the cold:

Large main compartment —for stuffing clothing removed, extra clothing, lunch, vacuum bottle, and other gear. (The small day pack used in other seasons is inadequate in winter.)

Coated nylon — waterproof bag designed so that minimum water will enter through zippers and other points.

Ample flap—should be large enough to completely cover main compartment opening.

External frame or other type of bag support —to keep bag away from the back, ventilate the space and prevent back wetting.

Outside pockets —for small items: first-aid kit, whistle, extra mittens, nibble food, nylon cord, etc.

Map compartment — easily accessible in pack flap or in rear of bag.

Padded shoulder straps—to reduce pressure on shoulders.

Simple bag closures —reliable, high quality plastic zippers on small pockets covered by rain guards; cord lock on main compartment drawstring. Spring-loaded buckle, or other easy functioning type, to secure cover strap.

Lash points—tough leather patches sewn on outside of bag for securing crampons, snowshoes, or other items.

Ice ax holder—if you intend to carry an ice ax.

Framepacks (also called backpacks) are available in many design varieties and makes, so that it is not a simple matter to make the best decision in purchasing one. Price is not necessarily a measure of good design and quality. But it is better to invest a little more to get superior equipment in lieu of the cheapest, poorly made framepack.

Winter features for packs, such as coated nylon fabric, for the most part apply also to framepacks. In addition, a framepack involves proper selection of frame size, total design, and consideration of principal features so that you will have the most comfortable unit with a full load.

50 EQUIPMENT

Winter backpacking in the Adirondacks.

These features are:

Frame — Proper size selection so that most of the load is supported by the hips and that the shoulder straps are secured at the optimum point on the frame—not too high nor too low in relation to the shoulders.

Hip belt — Whether location on the frame is adjustable, whether belt is padded or unpadded, and whether belt is one-piece or two pieces. The single-piece, padded belt seems to be favored on account of better support. If your purchase was a two-piece, unpadded belt, you may be able to install a single-piece, padded belt. Your layers of clothing provide padding, so this feature in winter is probably not important. Also there is some weight saving.

Back band—Can be either one-piece wide mesh, nylon fabric bands, or of narrow pads. All should be securely adjustable to the best position on the frame. The padded type is not favored, leaving your choice to one of the other two types.

Shoulder straps — Sufficiently wide and adjustable as to length and position on the frame for comfortable support. Straps should be long enough to fit around maximum clothing thickness.

Lashing studs, hooks or D-rings—Attached to frame for quickly securing snowshoes, crampons, tent poles, etc. outside the bag.

Not everyone, especially teenagers, will have "spending money" to invest in a good framepack. A little ingenuity and resourcefulness can solve the problem and permit enjoyable winter trips.

Purchase just the pack frame, then plan to get the bag later. In the meantime one can secure various combinations of bags, or a pack, or both, directly to the frame.

Another option is to make a wooden packframe in the home shop. One design is shown in Fig. 19. Other designs of homemade frames are detailed in the Bibliography [31, 37].

Ski backpacking requires unique features in a pack: close support by the body yet allowing free body movement, low center of weight, yet capable of carrying a sleeping bag and other essentials for at least two days. A framepack is of course a top-heavy, rigid system that is fine for walking, not skiing. The alternatives are to use the framepack anyway despite its drawbacks; lower the bag on the frame and place heavy items in the bottom half of the bag and next to the body; use the best available, new type, hip-supporting pack—frameless or with

52   EQUIPMENT

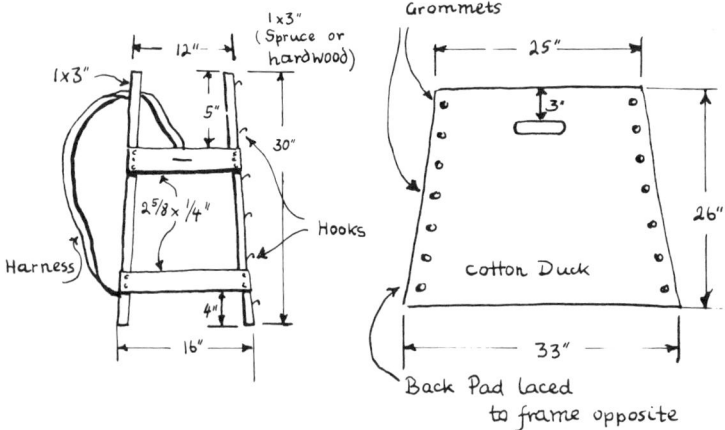

Fig. 19 — Design for a homemade packframe. (For clarity, in drawing at left only half of harness is shown.)

internal stays—such as the Jensen pack, Jansport Frame Sack, Lowe Expedition, and the North Face Kaksack; or use the latest type of large, shoulder-supported pack with various types of battens or stays, like the Bergans, Karimoor, and Millet. If you can't choose any of these, buy or borrow an old Army rucksack and do the best you can with it.

SLEEPING BAGS

The selection of an adequate sleeping bag is essentially a compromise between warmth and weight. The need for warmth may mean exceeding the total allowable weight of the pack load. If the trip involves transportation of supplies and equipment by private car to a starting point, one can afford the luxury of more and heavier equipment, at least as far as the roadside encampment. Here we concentrate on the backpacker's problem: "the most for the least."

The basic function of the sleeping bag is to allow safe and comfortable sleeping in the cold—and, if necessary, to reduce body heat loss by an injured member of the party. The bag's effectiveness depends on insulation, made possible by air spaces. Ideally the bag should provide a uniform insulating thickness around the body. Air space between body and bag is important. Too much space means increased surging and air circulation; too little space makes an uncomfortable bag, difficult to get into and out of, with less insulation.

The mummy-shaped bag—all down or polyester filament, or combination—is recommended from the standpoint of warmth and weight. Type of wall construction, quality of insulation (filling power), bag fabric, sewing, zipper, and hood details—all are important features of a well-made and quality bag.

Warmth of bag is mostly determined by bulking quality—ability to maintain large volume under low pressure, also called "filling power" and "loft"—of the insulation. Latter must be highly compressible so that the bag can be stuffed into a small sack. Slapping and shaking the bag after pulling it out will fluff it up again to maximum loft.

The most expensive item in a down sleeping bag is the insulation. The best quality down has the greatest filling power, which generally is goose down; duck down is generally lower. A purchaser has no simple way of knowing down quality in a particular bag. Bag manufacturers are not required to specify down quality on labels in terms of filling power. A buyer must depend on the reputation of the manufacturer and dealer. In any case, inquiry should be made of the loft measurements—whether goose, duck or mixture—for a particular brand and type of bag.

There are indications that down supply from abroad is not as good as formerly. That factor plus increased demand, it is said, has resulted in lower grades for sleeping bags. For many winter trips, if cold is moderate, it is not necessary to have the most expensive bag with the highest-lofting down possible. This would be expensive and the bag can be used only in cold weather.

In a well-made bag the zipper is backed by a down tube, or otherwise insulated, so that heat loss through the zipper is minimized. Because of this tube the zipper slide can frequently be jammed by the tube fabric. A good bag would also have a nylon (not metal) double-sliding zipper, which can be zipped from either the top or the bottom. To reduce leakage around the head, the closure—usually with a drawstring—should be designed for a tight seal around the face.

With respect to the inner and outer shells of a bag, there are two schools of thought in design. One says the outer should be larger than the inner in diameter. The idea is to prevent cold spots which would otherwise result by the inner layer pressing against the outer. This is the so-called differential cut. The other school, advocating the space filler cut, says that the inner layer of the same diameter should closely fit around the sleeper's body, so that there are no pockets of circulating air.

Bags are commonly made with shells of nylon material — tough, lightweight, downproof (to prevent leakage), and breathable (allows body moisture to penetrate). Nylon also has a slippery quality that allows easy entry and exit, and the shell does not tend to adhere to the body while sleeping. While on the subject of shells, it must be noted that it is inadvisable to use any waterproof outer shell or other supplementary cover, such as rainwear or plastic sheet, over a sleeping bag, as body moisture escaping through the bag will inevitably condense on the inside surface of such cover.

However, a light-weight, waterproof stuff bag must be used for containing and keeping your bag dry en route.

You can increase a bag's warmth by wearing dry insulated underwear or other dry garments, such as a down jacket, or by using the two-bag system. Do not depend on getting additional warmth by wearing your hiking clothes. They may contain a lot of moisture, and, actually, little insulation is added. However, it is very awkward to completely remove and put on clothing in a small tent. So, to be practical, at least remove your pants. You will be more comfortable without them.

The bottom of the bag, with a body in it, is under a pressure of about 3 lb. per sq. in.—more than down can resist. Hence the bottom of the bag is but a thin insulating layer, through which about 50% of body heat is lost. Additional insulation is needed, such as an Ensolite or other foam pad over an air mattress, a thick foam pad by itself, or extra clothing.

Wall construction design (Fig. 20 for down bags) is intended to hold insulation in place in a uniform thickness. In an inferior bag the insulation shifts and causes heat loss through thin spots. According to *Backpacker* magazine, baffle design has these effects:

Box construction — "had tendency to allow the down to fall away from the baffles so that, in effect, you end up with not much more than a sewn-through pattern, resulting in cold spots."

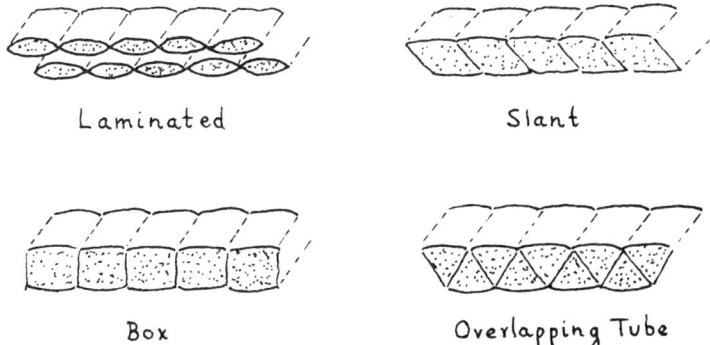

Fig. 20 — Wall construction of down sleeping bags in cross section.

Slant-wall construction—"is very popular because of its success in limiting down movement while at the same time allowing a bag to expand to its full lofting capacity."

Over-lapping tube—"requires more baffling than slant wall. As a result it is heavier and more expensive. However, it is a very efficient pattern for eliminating down shift."

Laminated — "Because this construction requires four layers of fabric it tends to make the bags heavy.

"Many bags also feature a so-called sidewall baffle opposite the zipper and running the entire bag length. This baffle is intended to prevent down shifting from the top to the bottom of the bag."

An effective way to solve the extra-warmth problem is to use two bags: a light-weight summer bag (1 lb. of down) inside a warmer bag with at least 2½ lbs. of down. The cost may be less, since you probably already have a lightweight bag for use at other times of the year. This combination has been used on expeditions as far as a base camp, to which the extra weight can be managed.

The Army uses a two-bag system for use in intermediate cold (cold-wet) and extreme cold (cold-dry) conditions. It appears that the bags are to be used separately. The first is for temperatures down to 10°F, the second below 10°F. The former bag is composed of an inner layer of polyester filament and an outer layer of 50% feathers and 50% down. The latter bag uses an inner layer of thicker polyester filament plus an outer layer of 100% down.

Can any bag keep a person warm at 20 below? Since persons differ greatly in basal metabolism (heat produced at complete rest), the answer depends on who is in the bag. Experimental data is meager as to the effectiveness of various type of bags at various temperatures. According to one calculation on the basis of tests, a bag with 7 clo of insulation (one clo is about equal to a business suit) will protect a man for 6 hours at 30 below. This assumes the man is warm when he gets into the bag. If he does not have this reserve heat—that is, if he loses heat as fast as it is produced by his metabolism—thicker insulation is required. The best bag tested gave "about 12 clo protection, enough to maintain thermal equilibrium at a temperature no lower than −20°F (−29.1°C)."[9]

Follow this rule of thumb, then: For below-zero temperatures a bag not less than 3 lb. (1.4 kg.) of down, or other insulation equivalent, should be used.

Polyester synthetic insulating filament, such as DuPont's Fiberfill II (Fig. 21) and Celanese's PolarGuard, is in common use for sleeping bags and garments. Fiberfill II consists of 2-inch hollow core fibers treated with silicone and must be enclosed in a nonwoven synthetic material to prevent leakage and shifting. PolarGuard is a continuous-filament fiber that is enclosed in batts coated with acrylic resin. Hollowbond II, a continuous filament similar to PolarGuard and a joint development of DuPont and E. L. Carpenter, is assembled into batts sprayed with a resin to give them shape. It appears that there is no substantial difference in insulating protection between these fibers. Polyester filament compares to down in the following respects:

1. Highly compressible, but about 90% as good as goose down; recovers quickly and has excellent insulating value. But compared to goose down, about 1.4 pounds of filament is required to equal the insulating value of 1 pound of down.
2. Dries quickly since filament absorbs less moisture than down.
3. Can be washed and dried with home equipment.
4. Durable, non-allergic, odorless. Down, with care, has these qualities also.
5. Retains much insulating value when wet. Decrease in loft is significantly less than down.
6. Cheaper.

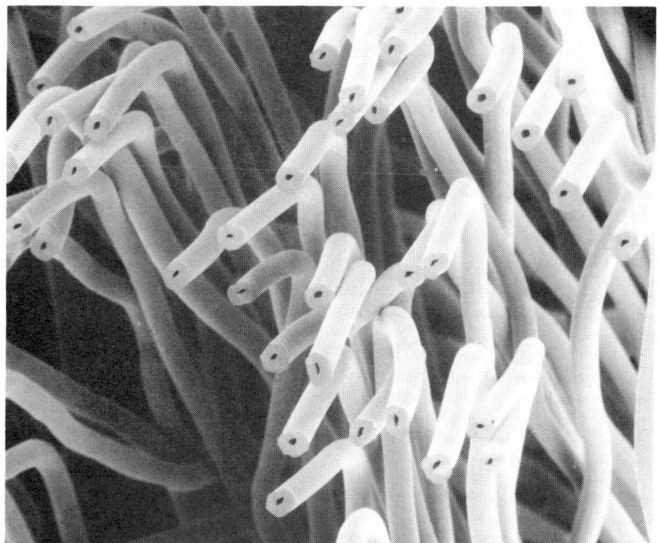

Fig. 21 — Micro-photo of Dacron polyester Fiberfill II showing hollow core filaments.

A new synthetic filament microfiber, Thinsulate, is made by combining polyester and polyolefin fibers and is a product of the 3M Company. Reported features include less bulk (about ½) and weight than other synthetic fibers, and resiliency when wet. Its principal use thus far is in garments.

A filament bag will be about 40% heavier and 20%–30% greater in bulk than an equivalent down bag. But a filament bag is cheaper, requires less care, and makes some sleep possible. Some hikers tend to be careless with their equipment, unnecessarily get themselves wet and do not adequately protect the sleeping bag. A filament bag for them would probably be the best choice. In any case, every hiker must take every precaution not to get the bag wet, whether down or filament.

The best filament bags are formed of two layers of staggered quilts. Loft throughout the bag should be uniform.

There are two ways to clean a down bag: dry cleaning and hand washing. Down will accumulate oils, odors and other material from your body and camping surroundings. It is important to clean your bag now and then, but not too frequently. Some filling power will be lost each time, so it is important to soil the bag as little as possible. (A flannel or nylon liner can be used to prevent soiling, but from the standpoint of weight saving, this is one item that can be left at home.)

The following cleaning instructions are from *Backpacker* magazine:

Dry Cleaning

1. Get cleaning done through a reliable outdoor equipment store where the staff is familiar with the subject and knows how it should be done to avoid damaging the bag.
2. The cleaner must be experienced in cleaning bags and one who uses a mild petroleum-based cleaning agent that is not harmful to down.
3. Air the bag for at least one week after it is returned to be sure all cleaning agent odors are removed. A bag inhabitant could otherwise get a skin rash from the cleaning agent. Continue airing until all traces are gone.

Hand Washing

1. Use lukewarm water in a bath tub, just enough to cover bag —a few inches. Use only Ivory flakes or a specially prepared down soap. Do not use a detergent.
2. Knead bag gently with your open hands; don't twist or wring. Drain tub and rinse bag. Repeat process until suds stay white—two or three times at most.
3. Rinse thoroughly last time to remove any remaining soap. Press bag firmly but gently to remove as much water as possible.
4. Pick up bag carefully, providing as much underneath support with your hands and arms as possible. Then take to a laundry which uses a large tumbler dryer.
5. Check dryer for any foreign objects and for any protrusions or sharp edges on the drum. Insert a pair of clean canvas shoes without laces. These are intended to break up down as it dries; rubber will produce some static electricity to help renew loft. Run dryer as many times as necessary to complete drying.
6. Finish with long airing in the sun.

In some respects, suppliers' instructions and opinions regarding cleaning differ with the above. One, for example, does not advise hand washing at all on account of likely damage to the bag. He also advises washing in a front-loading commercial washing machine, including use of a detergent.

Air your bag thoroughly after use. Then store it loosely folded in a clean, dry place. Remember:

1. Keep your bag dry. A damp bag is a cold bag.
2. Do not breathe inside the bag: this will dampen it.
3. Keep your bag clean.
4. Be sure to place extra insulation underneath.

Pads and Air Mattresses

Most backpackers today use foam pads rather than air mattresses. Some outfitters don't even stock air mattresses. In any case, your choices for winter camping consist of closed cell or open cell foam pads, or an air mattress supplemented by a closed cell pad. If necessary one can also use extra clothing for insulation. If you want deluxe comfort, try a ½" closed cell pad on top of an air mattress. It has been estimated that the closed cell pad—waterproof and less expensive than the open cell pad—is useful down to −20°F. Two inches of open cell foam, which absorbs moisture and therefore in some models is covered with a waterproof fabric, provides about equivalent insulation.

CRAMPONS

For serious snow and ice climbing—and even for a short trip to an ice-covered summit—good crampons are essential. Instep crampons may be adequate for a short distance, but for continuous, rugged use get a full-size pair.

Crampons are not too secure on a flexible boot, such as the all-rubber or the rubber-bottom, leather-top type. If such boots have rigid soles, the security is much better, but don't engage in any severe technical climbing. Use them for short stretches, but don't be surprised if they come off. Crampons for any boots, rubber or leather, must be fitted carefully in the shop when purchased. Adjustable crampons are obtainable, but use them only if adjustability is essential.

Choice of a particular type of crampon for a trip is at best a compromise between a number of desirable characteristics, such as footing security and ease of walking. For climbing iced

60   EQUIPMENT

On nearly level iced surfaces crampons make travel possible.

Using crampons on a steep slope.

peaks in New York and New England a 10-point crampon with about 1¾-in. points is satisfactory for most situations, giving security without allowing too much snow to ball up under the foot.

Makes and types include Grivel, Eckenstein, Ralling, Chouinard, Charles Moser adjustable, Simond Everest and Simon Grepon. Crampons are forged of charcoal or double-refined iron, galvanized steel, chrome-nickel steel (cadmium-plated), and other special steels. Points of steel crampons may fatigue, become brittle, and finally break under strain. If points of steel crampons are tempered excessively, they are likely to bend and become hazardous.

Keep crampon points sharp; otherwise your climbing will be more difficult. Sharpen points with a file, not a grindstone. Do not straighten bent points by hammering; they might snap. Take your crampons to a machinist or mechanic and ask him to straighten the points after heating with a torch.

Crampons are usually secured to the boots with either a single strap or two straps, one across the toe and through the four front rings, the second around the ankle and through the two rear rings. Since a strap may break, carry an extra—either web or leather.

When crampons are being carried, the points should be covered. One-piece rubber protectors are available; or carry the crampons in a canvas bag. As a last resort, wrap them in a garment in the pack and stow them with points facing the rear. Crampons lashed outside the pack are convenient, but dangerous to the hiker and to others; don't carry them this way unless the points are protected. Rubber crampon guards have been reported to freeze to the points if moisture gets under guards. To avoid this, remove guards at the trail head and fasten crampons to back of pack with a snap buckle and 1/16 inch polyethylene sheet to protect the pack.

ICE AXES

For negotiating steep trails or pitches and to assist in belaying, a good ice ax is essential. A reasonably priced, lightweight type is usually adequate for winter mountaineering. The ax should be long enough so that when you are standing it will reach from the floor to your wrist. If possible, rent or borrow an ax for a trip or two before buying one. The wrong length will tire you.

62   EQUIPMENT

Proper ways to carry the ice ax are shown in Fig. 59.

To prevent loss of an ice ax, use a looped cord, one end secured to the ice ax head, the other to a breakaway loop on your wind pants, the line just long enough to permit use at the farthest extension. When the line is not needed, it is detached from the head and stuffed inside wind pants leg via the unzipped fly. Tape should be applied to the ax head to prevent skin from freezing to the steel.

SNOWSHOES

Types of Snowshoes

Snowshoes for steep trails and bushwhacking in mountain country need to be short and sturdy, useful for kicking steps in the snow on the ascent, and of a size convenient for lashing to a pack. In relatively flat, treeless country the long trail-type snowshoes, such as Cross Country or Michigan, may be

Chippewa Indian on snowshoes, about 1900.

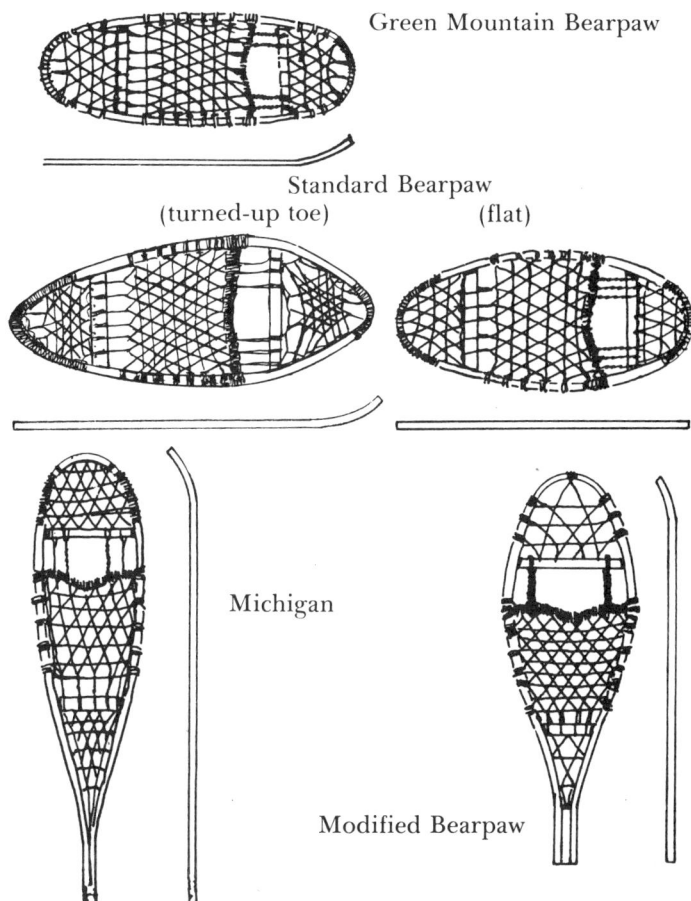

Fig. 22 — Types of wooden snowshoes for the mountains.

superior. A number of different designs suitable for steep climbing in New York and New England, including aluminum and plastic types, are available:

Green Mountain bearpaw (wood): Narrow shoe, rounded tail, toe turned up. Walking and edging easier on side slopes; more surface on rounded tail. Turned-up toe facilitates descent.

"Lightfoot" and "Tracker" (aluminum): Short, narrow, sharply turned-up toes, no cross bars, and with "decking" instead of

lacing for flotation. Features hinge-pin binding with integral traction plate.

Modified bearpaw (wood): Short, wide shoe with beavertail and turned-up toe.

Standard bearpaw (wood): Short, wide shoe with turned-up toe and round tail.

Some brands include the flat bearpaw, which makes climbing easier but toes tend to dig in on descent. Flat shoes also make a compact bundle on the pack.

Among the aluminum snowshoes on the market is the "Sherpa" (Fig. 23). Features include narrow, parallel aircraft grade aluminum frame without cross bars (in the short models), sharply turned-up toes, neoprene coated nylon (NCN) lacing and "decking" (NCN sheeting filling bulk of frame space), and binding position closer to the toe. Tracker 9 × 34 inch model, approximately equal in flotation and shape to the wooden Green Mountain (also the Cascade made to accommodate the binding), is about 10% lighter—about ½ pound. Width ranges from 9 to 10½ inches in four other models. Cost of Sherpa "Lightfoot" and binding would be about 50% greater than for Green Mountain bearpaw with binding; cost of "Tracker" and binding would be also significantly greater. Snowshoe and binding kits are available at a cost comparable to wooden snowshoes and other types of bindings. Cost can be lowered by using the wooden Cascade (Tubbs) model, with its binding position located nearer the toe, and the Sherpa hinge-rod binding.

In addition to lighter weight and durability, the manufacturer stresses simple, quick maintenance, better "edging" when moving laterally along a slope, greater efficiency of a small snowshoe in deep powder snow, and the advantages of their hinge-rod binding when used with a leather climbing boot.

The Sherpa snowshoe-binding combination appears to provide good traction and control, an essential requirement in steep mountain areas. However, an independent test and evaluation, based on conditions in New York and New England, is needed.

Plastic (polyethylene or polypropylene) snowshoes, lighter and less expensive than wooden ones, are preferred by some hikers. Cost, of course, is the deciding factor for many. Some hikers find a particular type just as effective for their use as a comparable wooden type. Their light weight should also be a

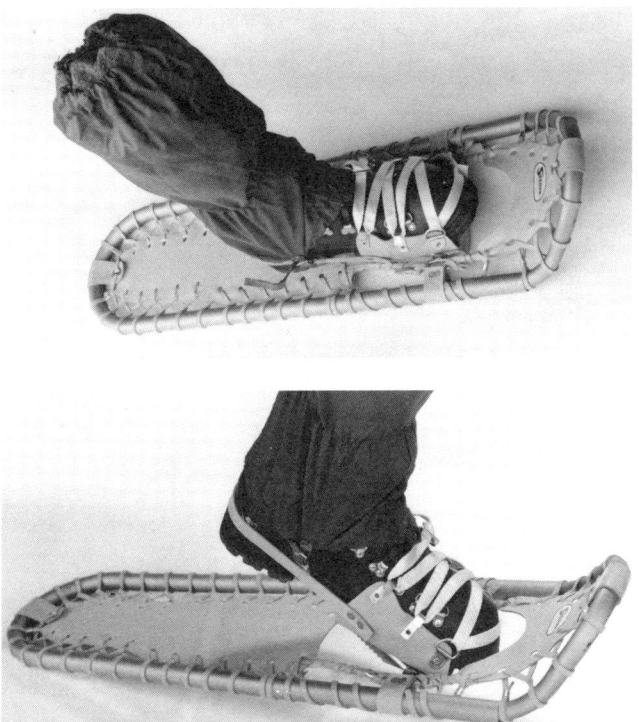

Fig. 23—Sherpa aluminum snowshoe and hinge-pin binding.

consideration. Some makes come with an inadequate binding, which should be replaced with one of the better types. Actual tests of particular makes and designs should be made to determine durability and other qualities.

Small plastic snowshoes have a particular use during early spring when snow may be encountered only on or near mountain tops. A pair can easily be carried on the pack until they are needed.

Many makes of snowshoes have neoprene-coated nylon lacing. It is lighter, picks up less snow, absorbs less water, and is easier to repair than rawhide. To prevent rawhide lacing from picking up wet snow, apply a coat of ski wax.

Unnecessarily heavy snowshoes waste energy and hasten the onset of fatigue. In choosing shoe size consider your weight

66 EQUIPMENT

(including pack load), your stride (height), and the depth and type of snow likely to be encountered. The Snowshoe Guide (Table 3) may be helpful in selecting the most suitable size and type.

A climber may want to attach spikes and angles to the bottom of his snowshoes to prevent slipping on crusty snow or icy patches. Specially made types are obtainable, but "homemade" varieties are not difficult to fashion. A pair of stamped instep crampons (with strap ring removed and side support flattened) can be lashed with rawhide to the bottom of each shoe. For better traction one can also use the halves of an old crampon.

Snowshoes laced with rawhide can be repaired by the manufacturer or yourself. Contact the maker of your snowshoes to obtain clarified rawhide. Request lacing of the proper width, depending on the part needing repair. After soaking the lacing in hot water, remove the broken piece and tie the new one in place under tension. When dry, apply at least two coats of exterior varnish.

Neoprene-coated nylon webbing in various widths may be available from some mountaineering-equipment supply houses.

Snowshoe Bindings

The ideal snowshoe binding should (1) be able to take the heavy strains encountered on ascent and descent, (2) keep the feet in the binding in all situations, (3) be easy to put on and take off, and (4) be easily repaired on the trail. Most commonly used types, frequently made of neoprene-coated nylon, are the H, Howe, and variations of the Howe, such as the Beck.

The H binding, which has no toe or heel piece, is easy to repair and adjust. On descent, however, considerable strain is felt on the instep if one is wearing flexible rubber-bottom boots.

The Howe binding has some superior features. It has a toepiece that takes up more of the strain and prevents the foot from slipping forward on the descent. It also has a wide heel piece and a pair of additional side straps to prevent twisting. It can be used with larger boots such as the all-rubber insulated type.

Fig. 24 shows some details of the Sherpa binding. A three-direction traction plate, to prevent slippage on crusts and icy

TABLE 3

Snowshoe Guide

(Size in inches; weight per pair, lbs., in parenthesis)

	Less than 4.5 lbs.	4.5 lbs. and over
For use in forested mountain country:		
Wood (Snocraft)		
Modified bearpaw (with beavertail)	11 × 32(3), 12 × 34(4)	13 × 36(4.5), 14 × 36(5)
Standard bearpaw (up-turned toe)	12 × 28(4), 13 × 33(4.3)	13 × 28(4.5), 14 × 30(5), 15 × 30(5)
Green Mountain	10 × 36(4.3)	
Aluminum (Sherpa)		
"Featherweight"	8 × 25(2.5)	
"Lightfoot"	9 × 30(3.3)	
"Tracker"	9 × 34(3.8)	
"Big Foot"	10 × 37(4.1)	
Plastic (Sportsmen Products)		
Standard	12 × 29(2.8)	
For use in hilly or level open country:		
Wood (Snocraft)		
Michigan		13 × 48(6), 14 × 48(6)
Cross Country		10 × 46(4.8)
Aluminum (Sherpa)		
"Big Foot"	10 × 37(4.1)	
"Musher"	10.5 × 44(4.1)	
Plastic (Sportsmen Products)		
Cross Country		12 × 38(5)

Note: Indication of make does not imply endorsement or superior qualities in comparison to other makes. Table is a practical way of showing types of equipment. Weights are for both snowshoes without bindings. Total weight of 13 × 28 flat rawhide bearpaw snowshoes, bindings and uninsulated, rubber bottom boots is about 10 lbs. Snowtreads are made of Eastman tenite polypropylene, a high-impact, subzero plastic, according to manufacturer. Sizes are in inches; weights in parentheses are in pounds.

spots, is secured permanently to the bottom of binding body. The boot is secured by webbing passing through D-rings and around hooks on the body. Binding tension is adjusted by this webbing, not by the heel strap. It appears that it is not necessary to tighten the heel strap, once it is adjusted, as in other types of bindings.

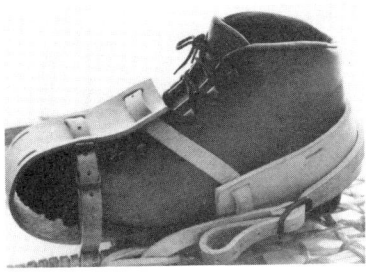

Howe binding

"K" binding

"H" binding

"Sherpa" binding

"F" binding

Fig. 24—Kinds of snowshoe bindings.

Before starting on an extensive trip, be sure to have a properly fitted binding that has been tested on shorter trips. Do not start for a summit with new, untried bindings. They may spoil the trip not only for you but for the rest of the party.

On a trip take a strap with a buckle and an extra-long rawhide lace to make a temporary binding (Fig. 25) if needed. Some veterans prefer to make repairs with wire. Your ability to make binding repairs may avoid a difficult "barefoot" retreat, perhaps in deep, soft snow.

70 EQUIPMENT

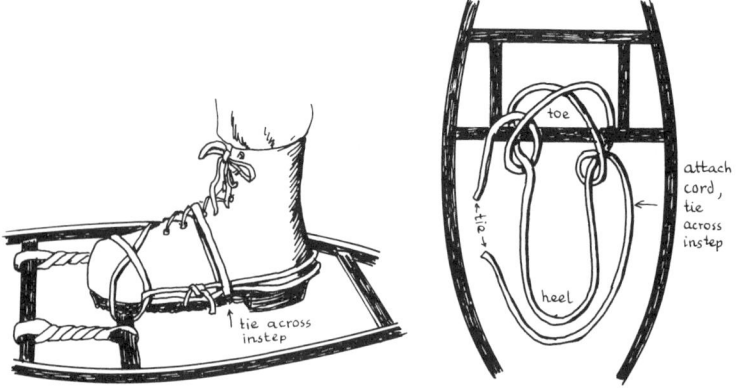

Fig. 25 —Emergency binding.

Poles

The climber on snowshoes generally uses ski poles or an ice ax. Steep pitches without either would make going difficult. If much ice is expected on the summit—perhaps involving technical climbing—the ice ax must be used. For deep snow a large basket can be fastened to the spike end of an ice ax.

One can get by with downhill, small-basket aluminum or fiberglass ski poles. If you can obtain a pair of thick, old-style bamboo ski poles with large baskets, they would be most appropriate for snowshoeing as well as being inexpensive. Bamboo can be handled with bare hands more comfortably, but it has a tendency to split rather than shear across. For increasing the surface area of your small-basket ski poles, you can install basket extenders.

SKI EQUIPMENT

Skis

Recreational skis suitable for cross-country travel—whether on groomed trails, unprepared forest trails, mountain climbs, golf courses or farms—come in three basic types: the light touring ski, the touring ski, and the mountain ski. In this book we are not concerned with racing skis, which are narrower, lighter,

Let's go!

and weaker than light touring and touring skis and are designed for maximum speed on a well-groomed track.

Light touring skis, with moderate flexibility and medium side cut, and weighing about 2 kilograms and measuring about 52 mm wide in the foot section, are intended to be used over prepared tracks and moderate terrain. Less energy is expended than would be with touring skis. Some makes have lignostone edges. Light touring skis are reported to be good in soft snow since a wider ski is heavier and more difficult to push through. Gain in flotation, which is determined mostly by ski length, is modest. According to Joe Pete Wilson, the light touring ski is the best for most people.

Touring skis are stronger and heavier than light touring skis, weigh about 2.2 kilograms, are about 53 mm wide, and have greater side cut for easier turning ability. Touring skis can be used on any kind of terrain, except perhaps icy and wind-packed snow areas of mountains, for which the mountain ski might be better.

Mountain skis are intended for back country and mountain use when one would want more rugged skis with steel or aluminum edges for control on ice or hard-packed snow. These skis are somewhat heavier than touring skis, have a width of about 60 mm, a relatively flat camber, tough bottoms

72 EQUIPMENT

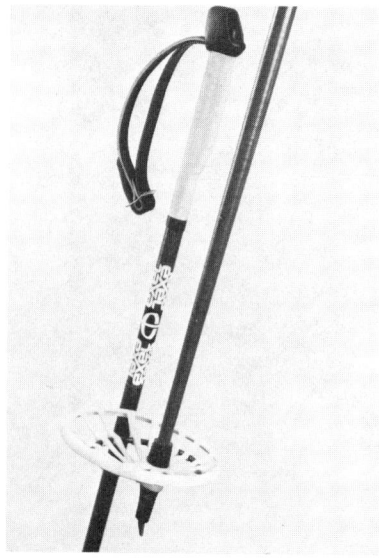

Fig. 26 —Carbon fiber mountaineering ski pole with large basket.

Fig. 27—Types of skis: (1) Downhill (2) Mountain (3) Touring (4) Light touring (5) Racing

to resist cuts and wear, and sufficient flexibility for easy turning and maneuvering. It has been stated that mountain skis are not necessary and that touring skis would perform satisfactorily for most ski trips, including backpacking, in the New York-New England area. However, there is still the possibility that mountain skis would be a better choice after closely considering terrain, snow and ice conditions, and other factors affecting a particular trip.

The terms "flexibility," "camber," and "side cut" should be explained. Flexibility and camber are jointly functioning features of a ski. The former refers to the stiffness in the overall ski, that is, the degree to which the tip and tail bend in relation to the thick middle section. Too flexible a ski means excessive wear on the midsection and excessive drag during glide. Flexibility also affects tracking and turning ability in loose snow.

Side cut, or the inward curve of the side of the ski, with the narrowest point in the binding area, is a feature that affects easier turning when compared to skis with straight sides. As a ski enters soft snow on a turn, for example, and as the tip bites into the snow, the ski waist slides inward. The tail bites also but less than the tip.

Most waxable and waxless skis used today consist of various kinds of fiberglass construction with polyethylene bases. There are other types of skis made of synthetic materials, but for the purpose of this discussion the term "fiberglass'" shall be used for the former group.

The fiberglass ski has advantages over the all-wood ski. It does not require a base coating. The running wax can be applied directly to the base, although some advise first applying a hard, low-temperature wax. Fiberglass construction results in a stronger ski; it thus can be made lighter. Also, the fiberglass ski resists moisture penetration better, is tougher, and is easier to manufacture for specific qualities — a more flexible tip, for example.

The fiberglass ski, however, does have some drawbacks. It is in general more expensive than a wood ski. Unless the base has a running wax on it, the fiberglass ski will not grip at all, whereas the wood ski retains some gripping ability without a running wax. Unless the fiberglass ski is rewaxed when the previous coating has worn off, it becomes more difficult to ski.

Today waxless skis comprise as much as 50% of the U.S. market. Obviously, waxless skis remove the necessity to wax, a chore which many people find onerous, messy and frustrating. Waxless skis, however, are slower than waxable, and some types produce a rasping noise. None of the waxless types appear to perform effectively for all snow conditions, but they are convenient and work well where snow conditions change frequently. Whether one would be satisfied with waxless skis depends largely on skiing ability and expectations. In ski backpacking, speed is usually not important, downhill running may have to be cautious, and the plodding movements are often similar to snowshoeing. But those skiers looking for maximum performance in climbing and running might still prefer to use waxable skis even though they involve more preparation and maintenance.

If you are in doubt regarding the best ski for you, rent different types before buying.

In purchasing skis and poles Table 4 may be helpful in choosing proper lengths. A light person may use slightly shorter skis; a heavy person, slightly longer. Serious tourers wishing to ski fast may want a slightly longer ski.

Poles should reach to just above the armpits. Length can be shortened slightly by adjusting the strap. Poles are bamboo (tonkin cane), aluminum, or fiberglass; for deep snow they should have large baskets. But for many snow conditions, a 4½

TABLE 4
Ski/Pole Length Guide

| | Height | | Ski Length | Pole Length |
	Ft.	In.	(cm)	(cm)
Men	5	1	195	120
	5	3	200	125
	5	5	205	130
	5	7	210	135
	5	9	210	140
	5	11	210	145
	6	1	215	150
	6	3	220	155
Women	4	9	185	110
	4	11	185	115
	5	1	190	120
	5	3	190	125
	5	5	195	130
	5	7	200	135
	5	9	205	140

EQUIPMENT 75

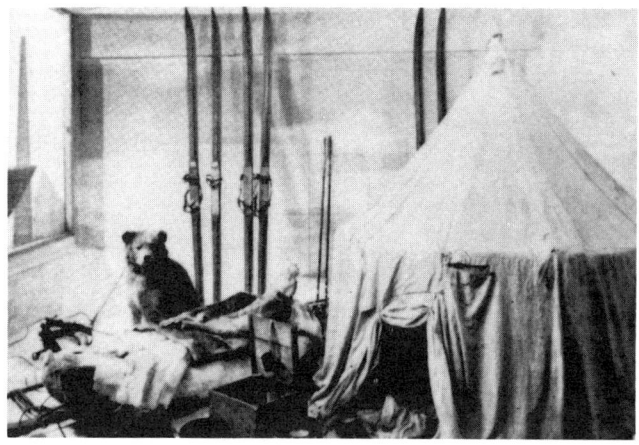

Type of conical, single pole tent used on 1910–1912 Antarctic Expedition and dash to South Pole, led by Roald Amundsen.

inch, 2-strap basket works well. Bamboo poles are popular on account of springiness and low cost. Usually they can be easily repaired by wrapping with tape. The pole tip is curved to ease withdrawal (the curve aims forward when holding the pole).

Ski Boots and Bindings

For ski touring, a boot-binding combination must allow the heel to move freely in the vertical plane from the base of the toes, but not relative to the ski in the horizontal plane.

Suitable boots include both high-cut and low-cut touring boots, the mountaineering boot and the military all-rubber insulated boot with a shelf at the heel.

Touring boots are offered both in a flexible-sole construction for use with pin-type bindings and in a reinforced-shank version for use with heel-cable bindings. The flexible-sole versions are also made low-cut to maximize the unrestricted forward bending at the ankle in the ski-touring stride.

Before the introduction of the serrated metal heel-plate the high-cut boot with the heavier sole design gave somewhat better downhill control, but with the general use of heel plates and other devices the advantage has largely disappeared.

76 EQUIPMENT

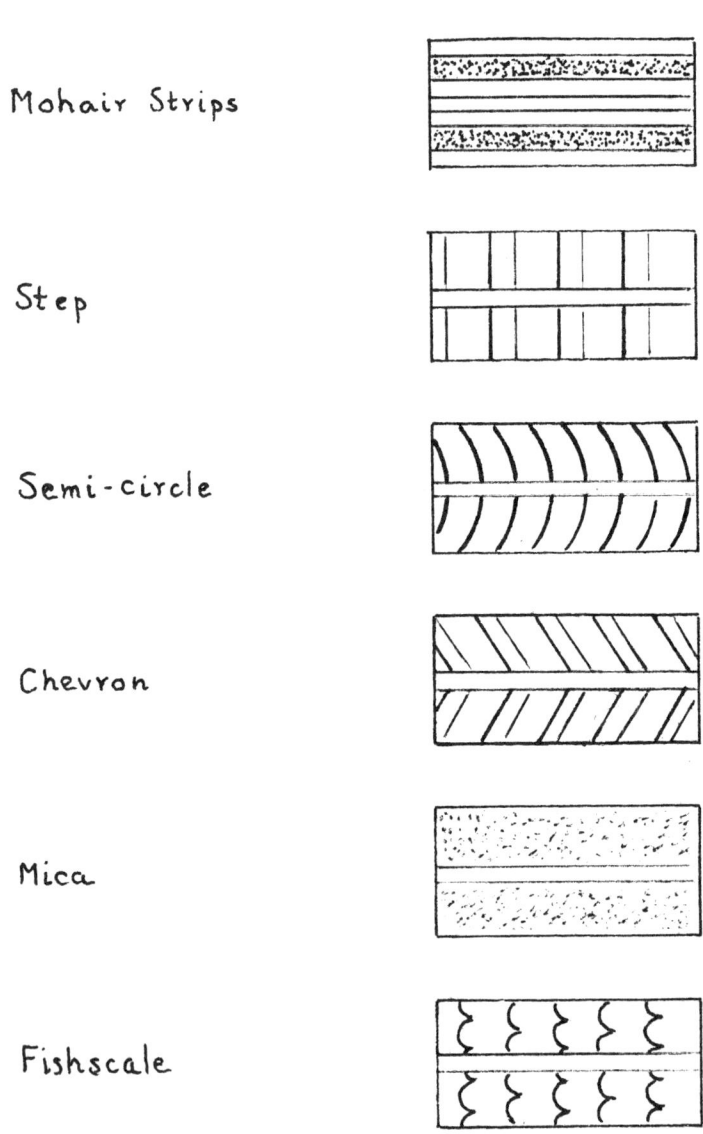

Fig. 28 — Waxless ski bases.

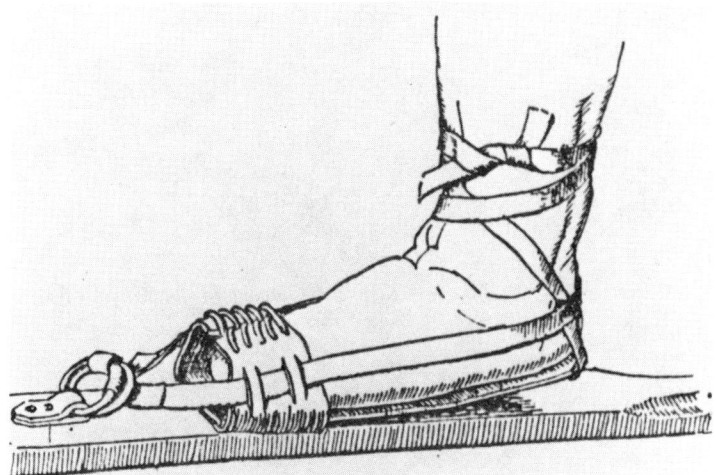

Fig. 29 — Experimental British binding for soft boots — about 1930.

The mountaineering boot with its roomy toe and lug sole may be used as a hiking boot with snowshoes and with crampons. The toe must have reasonably straight sides to be suitable for skiing.

A problem with ski boots is that they don't give sufficient cold protection. For the very best cold-weather protection consider the military all-rubber insulated boot. This means a considerable increase in weight and the need for special bindings like the military, all-terrain binding or the Uni-flex binding.

Low and high type gaiters may be used to keep snow out of ski boots and provide extra insulation. Insulated gaiters, booties, or socks may be used. A simple expedient is to carry in your pack a pair of wool socks large enough to fit over your ski boots when your feet start to feel cold. Insulated ski boots are available, but the amount of insulation appears to be modest. Gaiters may also be lined with soft felt, polyurethane, or Ensolite foam. Adding more material on the outside of the boot is much better than putting on more socks, which can retard circulation and make the feet more vulnerable to cold.

Bindings for touring and ski mountaineering are of two main types: the heel-strap or heel-cable binding and the pin-type binding.

78 EQUIPMENT

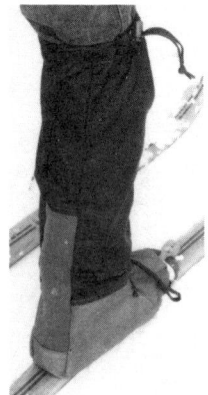

Fig. 30 — Insulated touring gaiter.

Fig. 31 — Insulated (½" foam) bootie for touring boots.

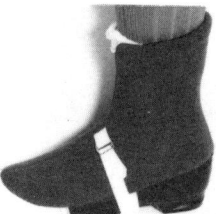

Fig. 32 — Touring boot sock.

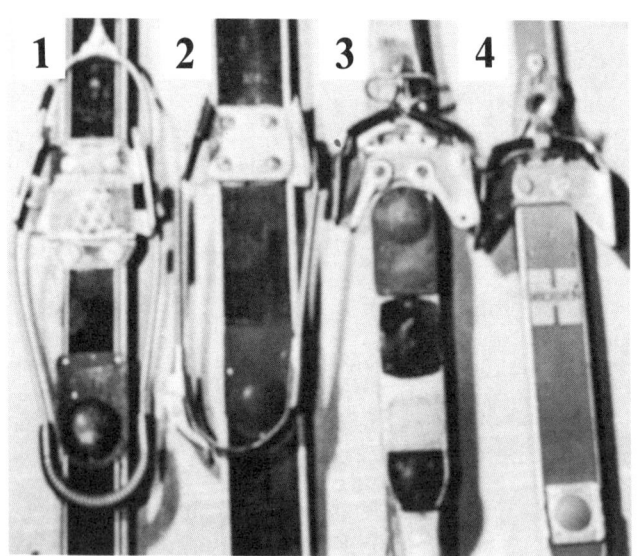

Fig. 33 — Types of ski bindings: (1) Cable binding (2) Heel-strap (Tempo) binding (3) and (4) Pin bindings

The former type, such as the Tempo, Gresshoppa, and Joffa, consists of a set of iron toe plates whose spacing is adjusted by interlocking teeth. In the latter two brands, a cable around the boot heel is tightened with an over-the-center toggle clamp screwed to the ski in front of the foot. The heel-strap (Tempo) binding uses a clamp around the heel and adjustable spring-like wire hooked to the side of the toe iron. A heel-cable binding commits one to use a fairly solid boot with a reinforced sole so that the sole does not buckle under the foot when tension is applied to the cable. Work shoes and hiking boots are often deficient in this respect because they ordinarily do not have a steel shank in the sole. It is also difficult to get work boots and hiking shoes to fit the toe irons properly.

A cable or heel-strap binding should not be adjusted or modified to prevent the heel from lifting. It is not unusual to run into a soft patch of snow or a drift and be thrown forward, face downward, in a full-length forward fall. If the heel can't leave the ski, a severe strain is put on the lower leg. It is imperative that the skier check his binding to be sure he can kneel down with the knee resting firmly on the ski with no sense of strain (Fig. 34).

Pin-type bindings are so called because of three upward projecting pins which engage holes drilled or molded into the boot sole. The boot is held on these pins with a bail which presses down on the sole at the front and is secured with a latch or notched catch. There is nothing to restrict the free upward

Fig. 34—Check the ski binding by kneeling on the ski.

80 EQUIPMENT

Fig. 35—Close-up of 3-pin binding. Secure boot by pushing down plate (with hole) under the latch with tip of ski pole. Release by depressing latch.

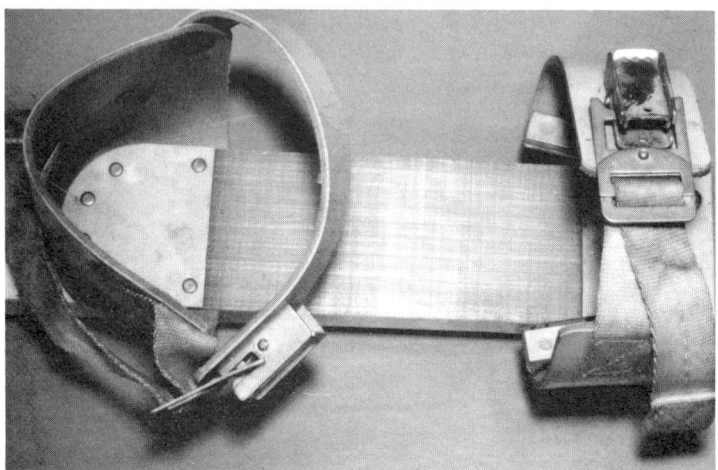

Fig. 36—Military, all-terrain binding.

EQUIPMENT 81

Fig. 37—Uni-flex (Bentley) ski binding.

rise of the heel, except the stiffness of the boot sole itself. Pin bindings demand the use of boots with flexible soles that can withstand bending. If a boot heavy enough for use with a heel-cable binding is used in a pin binding, the sole will bend severely under the ball of the foot, so that it may crack open in a season's use.

Around 1970 the three-pin binding was standardized so that suppliers could offer boots in a wide size range with pre-drilled holes that would fit any binding of any make. Common brands of pin bindings are Rottefella, Bergan, Skilom, Troll, and Villom, differing in the way the bail is latched.

In recent years the Uni-flex (Bentley) binding (similar to the military, all-terrain binding), with flexible plastic sole piece, toe bracket and strap, and heel support and strap, was introduced. This binding allows the use of a flexible-sole leather hiking boot or a rubber insulated boot as well as a conventional ski boot. By using a rubber insulated boot you get the cold protection that is substantially lacking in other boots. It is important to follow mounting instructions carefully so that the sole piece, when fastened to the ski, lies perfectly flat against the surface. Any burrs around drill holes or any other surface protrusions must be removed before mounting.

It is important to be able to release any binding easily with one hand. One may fall in such a position that the skis must be removed before getting up. The binding should release without a struggle. It may be necessary to file down the latches on some Rottefella bindings so that releasing can be done with moderate thumb pressure.

Serrated heel plates and similar devices fastened to the ski under the heel improve ski control when low-cut touring boots and pin bindings are used. Keeping the weight on the back of the foot causes the boot heel to engage the plate. The boots have strong heel counters so that the force required to steer the ski is transmitted at the rear end of the boot. This combination often gives adequate ski control comparable to that of the heavier boot-and-cable binding, improving freedom of motion and saving weight. However, snow and ice frequently and quickly adhere to heel plates, thus nullifying their effectiveness. Control can also be obtained by using heel locators—in effect a pin and slot mounted on the back of a touring boot and on the ski. When the boot is flat on the ski, the pin fits into the slot. The drawback of locators is that they do increase the risk of leg injury.

Choosing Ski Equipment

What of the relative merits of various types of skis, boots and bindings? Basically the choice is between the heavy and wide steel-edged mountain ski, the touring ski, and the light touring ski. The mountain ski is most frequently used with a cable binding, often with downhill hitches and a fully releasable binding, such as the Silvretta Saas-Fee or Ramy Securus. The touring ski may take either the heel cable binding or the pin binding. The light touring ski must be used with a pin binding because the screw hole spacing in most cable bindings will bring the screws too close to the edge.

The weight difference between mountain skis and the light touring outfit, including boots, may range from 4 to 6 lbs. Between touring skis with a cable binding and a light touring outfit the difference may be 3 to 4 lbs. A hiking rule of thumb says, "One pound on the feet is like five pounds on the back."

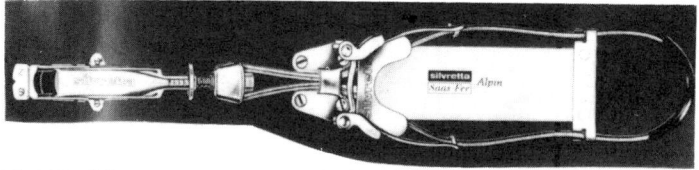

Fig. 38—Silvretta mountaineering binding.

The choice of heavier ski equipment is comparable to adding 15 to 25 lbs. (6.8 to 11.3 kg.) to the pack, so there is no question that lighter gear adds greatly to skiing enjoyment.

There are few locations in the northeastern United States where use of the mountain ski is really justified. The choice is reduced to the wider touring ski or the narrower light touring ski. For general forest use (rather than high mountain climbing) with occasional overnight camping, the touring ski probably would be a better choice.

TENTS

Basic Requirements

On a weekend backpacking trip one can take a single-fabric, lightweight mountain tent of the one-man or two-man type. At the cost of extra weight a double-walled tent will give greatly increased protection against cold. If backpacking is not involved, larger and heavier tents of assorted types and styles can be considered.

A tent provides basic shelter without the luxury of centralized heating. For warmth one must depend on extra clothing, sleeping bag, and a cook stove.

To retain heat, a tent, like clothing, must be in effect two tents, one inside the other—the dead air-space principle again. With a fitted fly reaching snugly to the tent floor, and a frost liner, a tent would have two dead air spaces. In addition to adding some insulation, a frost liner allows moisture-laden vapor to pass through to the inside of the tent roof where the vapor condenses into frost. When the tent is disturbed, the frost falls to the top of the liner and slides down the side instead of falling onto the tent's occupants.

84 EQUIPMENT

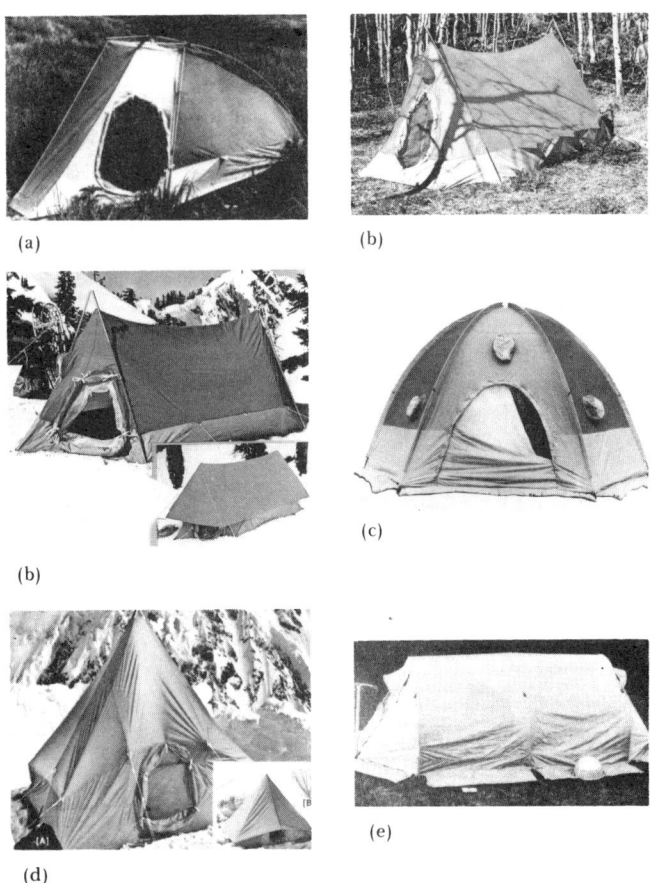

Fig. 39 —Types of winter tents: (a) External frame tent (b) "A" tents (c) Dome tent (d) Pyramidal tent (e) Tunnel tent

To withstand severe weather conditions and provide comfort, winter tents should have other characteristics:

High-strength fabric: Most quality small tents today are made of water repellent and mildew resistant nylon, although Dacron is claimed to be superior with respect to deterioration from ultraviolet rays. Tent fabric must be "breathable"—that is, allow air to pass through it. Resistance of the fabric to tearing and expansion under tension should be exceptional. To minimize flapping of panels and prevent squeezing of the interior space in high winds, the panels should be adequately secured by guy lines or braced by wands, or both. Corners, stake loops, guy loops, and webbing attachments should be reinforced; grommets should be in several layers of cloth; zippers should be double stitched.

High-angle roof: Snow will pile up on a tent with a low-angle roof—unless you get up in the middle of the night to shovel it off. You may have to dig yourself out in the morning anyway if there has been a 3-ft. snowfall or if drifting has occurred. The chance of a collapsed roof is less if the roof has a high angle.

Protected entrance: Tent entrances must be protected from incursions of snow and wind. A tunnel entrance is a common feature of winter tents, but getting in and out in bulky clothing may be somewhat awkward. Snow has to be beaten off clothing and equipment outside the tent. At the opposite end there may be a zipper opening. Two tents may be joined together.

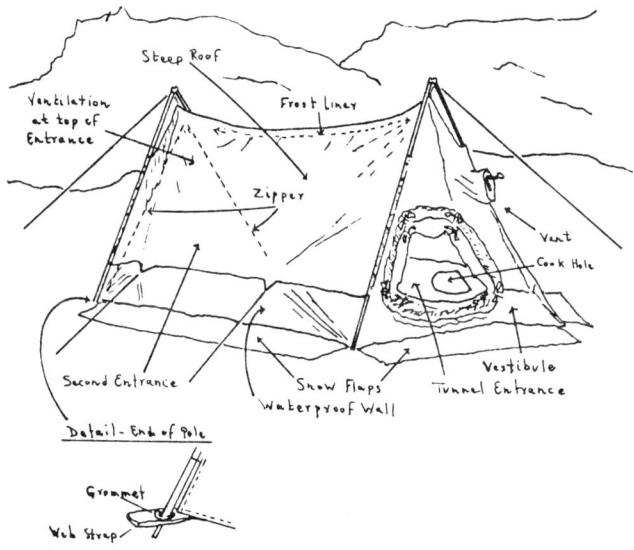

Fig. 40 —Features of a winter tent.

TABLE 5
Some Tents for Winter Camping

Make	Height (in.)	Dimensions (in.) Floor	Walls	Entrance
Bishop Ultimate (B)*	40	60 × 84	9	Zipper door (2)
Mountain II (G)	49	81 × 59	7	Zipper door, Tunnel
Expedition (H)	47	114 × 60	12	Zipper door, Tunnel
Mountain Dome (J)	52	84 × 96	22	Zipper door, Tunnel
Expedition Alpine (E)	49–19	96 × 60	13	Tunnel
Hexagon (S)	72	93–84 (hexagon)	13	Zipper door
St. Elias Expedition (N)	45	94 × 56	14	Zipper door, Tunnel
Tuolumne (N)	46	84 × 50	15	Tunnel
Crestline Expedition (R)	46	88 × 60	11	Zipper door, Tunnel
Expedition (P)	48	102 × 60	12	Zipper door, Tunnel
Snow Line II (Ba)	48	84 × 58	8	Zipper door, Tunnel
Fitzroy (Sk)	51	105 × 60	16	Zipper, Tunnel
Omnipotent (Ea)	38	87 × 54	5	Zipper
Glacier (S)	45	89 × 53	12	Zipper, Tunnel
Timberline (E)	56	89 × 63	12	Zipper
Camp 7 (C)	41	93 × 52	—	Zipper

*Letters indicate suppliers.

Suppliers Indicated by Key Letters in Table 5

R — Recreational Equipment, Inc.
G — Gerry
H — Holubar Mountaineering Ltd.
B — Bishop's Ultimate Outdoor Equipment
E — Eureka Tent, Inc.
J — Jansport

Snow Flaps	Weight (incl. Poles)	Vestibule	Capacity	Cook-Hole
No	10 lb. 8 oz.	No	2	No
No	7 lb. 10 oz. (incl. fly)	Yes	2	Yes
Yes	10 lb. 1 oz. (incl. fly and stakes)	Yes	2	Yes
Yes	10 lb. (incl. fly)	No	3	No
No	10 lb. 14 oz.	Yes	2	Yes
No	8 lb.	No	3	Yes
Yes	8 lb. 2 oz. (incl. fly and frostliner)	No	2	Yes
No	5 lb. 14 oz. (incl. fly)	No	2	No
No	8½ lb. (incl. fly)	Yes	2	Yes
No	11 lb. 7 oz. (incl. fly)	No	2	Yes
Yes	8 lb. 11 oz. (incl. fly)	Yes	2	Yes
No	8 lb. 5 oz. (incl. fly, stakes)	Yes	2	No
No	5 lb.	No	2	No
No	7 lb. 11 oz.	Yes	2	Yes
No	7 lb. 4 oz.	No	2	—
No	5 lb. 6 oz.	No	3	No

N — The North Face
P — Paul Petzoldt Wilderness Equipment
S — Sierra Designs
Ba — Eddie Bauer, Inc.
Sk — The Ski Hut
Ea — Early Winters, Ltd.
C — Camp 7

Waterproof floor: Mountaineering tents today have waterproofed, sewn-in floors. Floor material should extend up the sides 9 inches or more to prevent sleeping bags and other gear from getting wet. A zippered hole is provided in some designs near the entrance for a cook stove and getting rid of mess such as snow and spilled liquids.

Ventilation: Large vents must be provided in the top or ends of the tent to exhaust products of combustion from cooking and heating and to reduce the accumulation of hoarfrost.

Security against collapse: How does one secure the tent in soft, deep snow? A broad exterior flap called a valance—as wide as 24 in. in the larger sizes—along each side of the tent will do the job. After the tent is erected, place packed snow, ice blocks, and gear on the valance. If the snow hardens, it will hold firmly. Such snow can be used instead of ice and rocks. The weight of all this material plus snow stakes should ordinarily be enough to secure the tent.

LIGHTWEIGHT STOVES

Don't plan to use wood fires for cooking on winter hiking trips. They are too difficult to start and maintain under many weather conditions. Cooking takes too long, involving too much personal exposure and discomfort.

Take along some type of lightweight stove. The ideal one has these features:

High heating efficiency
Sturdy construction, yet lightweight
Safe fuel—no noxious lead fumes
Low carbon monoxide output
Simple, foolproof operation
Wind screen
Stability—not easily tipped over

The stove should have sufficient stability for a large pot. Some stoves have a narrow base and are easily knocked over. Be extremely careful while using such a stove in a tent or tent opening. Do not refill tank of a hot stove; fuel spilled on the burner may ignite! Never remove the tank cap while stove is operating! Be sure to put your fuel bottle a safe distance away from an operating stove! Be sure also that there is no spilled

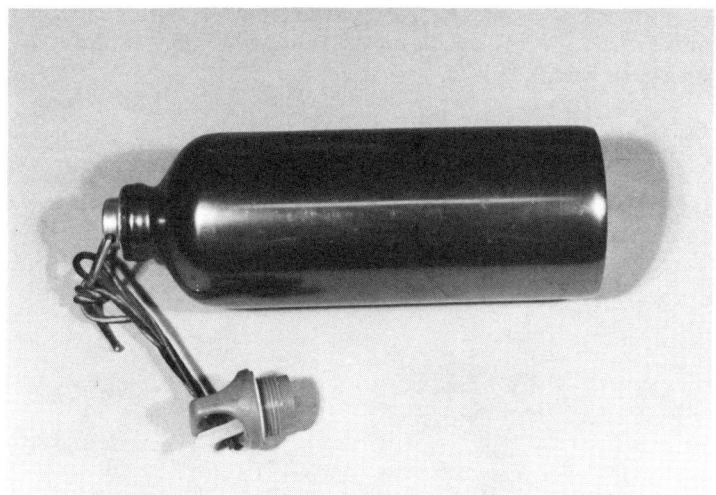

Fig. 41 —Fuel bottle with attached filler cap.

fuel on or around the stove before you ignite it! Use a heat resistant board under the stove. For a convenient match striker, glue a piece of sandpaper or emery cloth to the stove container.

Characteristics of some stoves suitable for winter use are given in Table 6. Study this data carefully if you are about to buy a stove with a particular trip in mind. Solidified-alcohol stoves can at best only heat previously prepared food, but may be suitable in mild weather.

Kerosene Stoves

For many years kerosene has been the preferred fuel in cold regions, but in recent years has been largely replaced by gasoline. Kerosene is much safer than gasoline—a prime consideration where cooking will be done in a tent or other enclosed shelter.

Tank pressure in a kerosene stove is provided by a built-in pump. The stove must be primed with alcohol or other volatile fuel, thus requiring more time to prepare a meal. Kerosene may be difficult to obtain, and its odor will be absorbed by clothing and skin.

90 EQUIPMENT

Double filtering of kerosene is advised for better performance. One hiker uses a plastic bottle, instead of aluminum, for his spare fuel.

Gasoline Stoves

Most self-generating and pump-generating gasoline stoves are designed to burn nonleaded fuel. However, some types will burn both leaded and nonleaded fuels. Fumes from the combustion of leaded gasoline can be injurious if inhaled; use only

Fig. 42—Optimus 111 (kerosene), 111B (gasoline); 8R (gasoline).

Fig. 43—Phoebus 625.

in a well-ventilated area. Nonleaded fuel intended for automobiles will produce carbon deposits that impair stove operation; it also will produce more carbon monoxide. A specially refined stove fuel will give less trouble. This gasoline will have a lower combustion temperature and will burn more completely with less unburned hydrocarbons and carbon monoxide.

A pump-generating stove can be started faster than others but is heavier because of the additional mechanism. The extra weight and bulk are offset by the facility with which a hot metal can be obtained in the extreme cold.

Fig. 44—Phoebus 725.

Fig. 45—MSR stove.

Fig. 46—Primus 2252 propane stove.

Both types of stoves require priming, but the self-generating stove is dependent on heat feedback for tank pressure. Primer gasoline can be extracted from a tank by using an eye dropper or a short piece of transparent tubing. In the case of the Optimus 8R stove, with its plastic knob on the control shaft, the shaft can be used for priming. Drill a hole in the knob and attach the chain there. Place your finger over the hole in the shaft to extract gasoline from the tank for priming. Getting the fuel to flow by warming the tank on a self-generating stove with the hands is not recommended in the cold. Fig. 47 shows the mini-pump which can be used on the Svea 123 and Optimus 8R, 80 and 99 stoves fitted with a special tank cap. Unless a self-generating stove is suitably protected from the wind, it will tend to lose pressure and the flame will die out. Even if suitably protected, it will not put out enough heat to boil water on extra cold days.

Canadian Army tests at −30°F and below of Coleman 1-burner and 2-burner stoves and the M1950 mountain stove markedly demonstrated the problem of starting and fuel burning once starting began. These stoves had generators which vaporized fuel prior to entering the nozzle and which required additional preheating before the stoves could operate satisfactorily.

A primer test, fully protected from the wind, was conducted outdoors at 44°F on the Optimus 111B (pump) and the Primus 71 (self-generating) stoves. Maximum height of flame results:

Primer	111B	71
Gasoline	19 in.	12 in.
Lighter fluid	16	10
Alcohol	12	9

The test is a strong indication that it is hazardous to use a gasoline primer inside a tent, not only on account of the flame height but also because gasoline ignites explosively. Lighter fluid (essentially naptha) and alcohol do not ignite explosively; the risk of burning the hand upon ignition is much less.

A stove should have a self-contained wind screen, or be set up in a tent, tent opening, or fixed shelter or behind some other protective barrier such as snow blocks or in a snow hole. Too much protection is not good either. The fuel tank can get too hot, causing the safety valve to pop and interrupting the meal schedule.

Some Stoves and Their Characteristics

Make and Model	Weight oz.[f]	Pump	Tank Capacity, fl. oz.	Maximum Burning Time, min.	Fuel	Boiling Time of 1Qt.[e] Water, min.	Dimensions, inches
Primus 71L	20	No	8	90	Gasoline	7–8	3½ × 3½ × 5¼[c]
Primus 71	10	No	5	45	Gasoline	8–10	3½ dia. × 4½ high
Primus 100	38	Yes	28	240	Kerosene	3–5[b]	8 dia. × 8 high
Primus 210L	35	Yes	16	120	Kerosene	3–5[b]	6¾ × 5¼ × 3½[c]
Primus 96L	30	Yes	8	120	Kerosene	6–7[b]	5½ × 5½ × 3¼[c]
Svea 121L	24	Yes	16	120	Kerosene	3–5[b]	9 × 8 × 4[c]
Primus-Pro 2252[i]	49	No	1.5	25	Propane/butane (40/60%), Propane (100%)	6	8 dia. × 4 (folded)
Svea 123R	18	No	6	45	Gasoline	6–7	3¾ dia. × 5 high
Optimus 80	20	No	8	90	Gasoline	7–8	3½ × 3½ × 5¼[c]
Optimus 96L	32	Yes	8	120	Kerosene	6–7[b]	5½ × 4½ × 3½[c]
Optimus 111B	56	Yes	16	90	Gasoline[d]	4–6[b]	6¾ × 6¾ × 4½[c]
Optimus 111	70[a]	Yes	16	90	Kerosene	4–6[b]	6¾ × 6¾ × 4½[c]
Optimus 77A	24	No	5.7	25	Alcohol	7½	8 dia. × 4½
Optimus 8R	26	No	5.3	75	Gasoline	7	5 × 5 × 3
Optimus 99[g]	23	No	5.3	75	Gasoline	7	5 × 5 × 3⅛
Baby Ender	22	Yes	4½	45	Gasoline	8[b]	4½ × 5¾ × 3[c]
Phoebus 625	40	Yes	16	150	Gasoline	3¾	5½ dia. × 7½
Phoebus 725	35	No	7.3	90	Gasoline	4	4¾ dia. × 4¼
Grass Hopper	12	No	27	360	Propane	9½	3¼ × 3¼ × 17
Gerry Mini Mark II	7¾	No	6	180	Butane	6½	4½ dia. × 5
Mountain Safety Research MSR G/K	16	Yes	16 & 32[h]	130	Gasoline, Kerosene, others	4	3½ × 3¼ × 9
Coleman Peak 1	31	Yes	10	210	Gasoline	3½	6½ × 4⅝

a Includes spirit can. b Depending on pressure. c Container size. d White or regular. e Indicates relative heat output, not absolute minutes at low temperatures. Field test at 22°F for boiling times for melted snow gave following results: Optimus 111B, 8 min.; Primus 71, 10 min. f Weight of fuel and heating efficiency also have to be considered. g Same as 8R except that 99 has aluminum cooking container. h Uses Sigg fuel bottles. i Tank can be filled from fuel cylinders; burning time (25 min.) is at full flame for 1 filling; includes 2 pots, windshield, 1 fry pan, grip handle, lighter, and filling adaptor.

94 EQUIPMENT

Extra gasoline or other liquid fuel can be carried in specially made metal bottles with neoprene gaskets. After filling the bottle be sure to check it for leakage that might contaminate your food and clothing. Stow the bottle in a plastic bag away from food.

Butane Stoves

One example of the butane stove is the Bleuet S-200. At above-freezing temperatures it has high heat output per unit weight and offers the advantage of quick starting. Butane has about 7% more energy than gasoline on a weight basis, 14% less on a volume basis. The stove does not have the continuous, even heat output of the gasoline or kerosene stove. When the tank is almost empty, output is about 30% of the initial amount.

At sea level the boiling point of butane is 31°F (−0.5°C), whereas at 25,000 ft. it's about −11°F (−24.1°C); performance therefore improves with increasing elevation. Unfortunately, its sensitivity to temperature change increases as fuel in the canister is consumed.

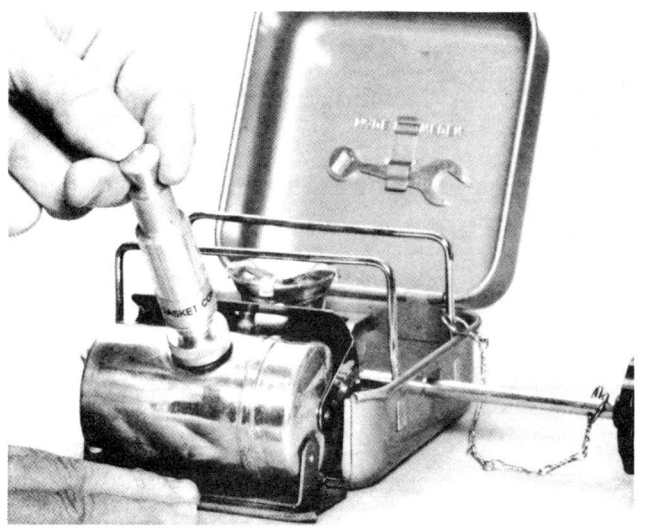

Fig. 47 — Pump accessory for self-pressurized stoves — shown on Optimus 8R.

TABLE 7
Heat Energy of Fuels

Fuel	Calories per Gram (approximate)
Kerosene	11,060
Gasoline	11,000
Butane	11,770
Alcohol: Ethyl	7,200
Methyl	5,300

In the low-elevation conditions of New York and New England mountainous areas the S-200 butane stove and others of the same type are not advisable. However, in recent years a new type of butane cartridge based on the liquid-feed principle was introduced by E. F. Industries and Optimus. The Gerry Mini Mark II, one such stove, does not depend on internal pressure to expel vapor from the cartridge as in the case of those makes using the vapor-feed principle, which depends on temperature. In the former system, the liquid butane is led out of the cartridge by an internal wick, so that conversion to vapor takes place outside the canister.[60]

COMPASSES

Many types and styles of compasses are shown in the equipment catalogs. Use a liquid-filled or induction-dampened compass—to give you a quick bearing—with a dial calibrated from zero to 360 degrees. With such a dial a direction can be measured to the nearest degree if the sighting is done with care. The compass should have a direction (lubber's) line for sighting on objects or for obtaining a reading on a map.

Some designs, such as the cruiser's or forester's compass, have a dial calibrated counterclockwise. East and west are transposed; north and south directions are unchanged. To get a direction, align the "north" end of the needle with the bearing in degrees. The zero point then indicates the desired direction. On a compass having a clockwise calibration one has to align zero with the "north" end of the needle. The desired direction is read off from that point. On the clockwise-calibrated compass, the rotating calibrated collar greatly simplifies direction reading.

96 EQUIPMENT

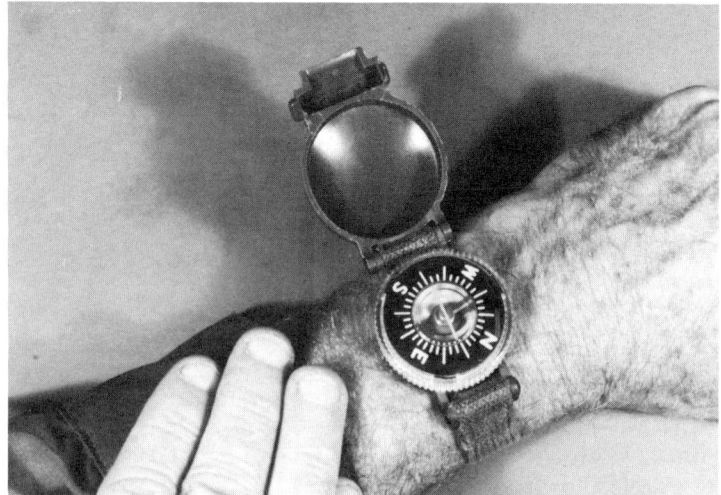

Fig. 48 — Wrist compass.

Lensatic compasses have a sighting eyepiece and a wire or notch front sight, coupled with a means of simultaneously reading the dial, either directly or on a mirror. This type of compass should be used when greater accuracy is required — for example, locating a point on a map by taking bearings to known points. For cross-country navigation, a compass with a direction line is sufficiently accurate.

In extreme cold it is possible for a liquid-filled compass to become inoperative because of inadequate clearance between the compass pin and its bearing. This does not happen often. In any case, keep your compass in a pocket or in the pack. For extreme situations take along an air compass as a spare.

Practice using your compass throughout the year. An excellent recreational as well as educational way is to participate in cross-country "orienteering" trips with your friends. These can be made as difficult and challenging as the skill of the participants will allow.

Ski Orienteering

According to Bjorn Kjellstrom, ski orienteering as a competitive sport is older than foot orienteering. Both were introduced in the U.S. in 1946. The first official ski orienteering races took place at Turin, N.Y., in 1948 and 1949. The ideal terrain for ski orienteering is a relatively open country network consisting of farms, woods, meadows, lakes, unused roads, and trails.

Ski orienteering can be in the form of point orienteering— following a route, which may be marked on maps, from point to point. Along such a route are secret control points which participants must mark on their maps. Risk of getting lost is minimal; novices can easily participate. Errors in pinpointing control points on maps are penalized by adding penalty time to running time. Another type of point orienteering features a skilled leader who escorts a group along a route with control points. As the competitors reach each point, they must mark the location on their maps. Penalties are imposed for deviating from the correct location. Compass and map instruction can be added if desired near the end of the tour.

In line orienteering, which is for the advanced, competitors follow a route which they have to copy from a master map onto their maps. If they follow the route correctly, they will also encounter control points. Each control station has a secret code number or letter, which must be noted by the competitors.

ALTIMETERS

An altimeter may be useful on a trip for indicating progress, especially in weather with low visibility. The instrument is used with a topographic map, which shows altitudes. Calibration should be checked and adjusted, if necessary, when you know exactly where you are and thus can read the altitude from the topo map. As weather changes, atmospheric pressure also changes, and recalibration is necessary.

SLEDS

Figs. 49 and 51 show sled types useful for hauling gear and supplies rather than depending entirely on backpacking. The child pulk, a boat-like sled, in Fig. 51 makes a family ski tour possible. Larger pulk models for cargo and rescue are available. On some public lands the use of sleds and toboggans is prohibited, so check the applicable regulations.

98 EQUIPMENT

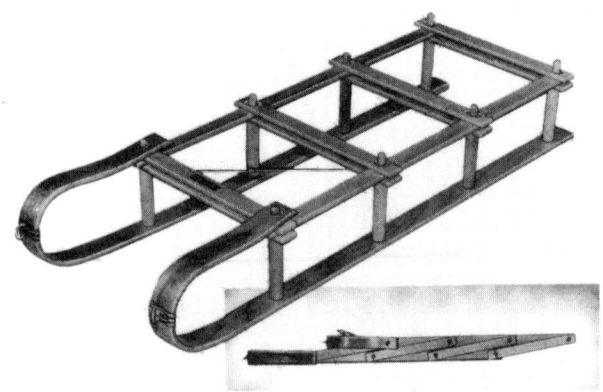

Fig. 49 — Folding sled.

Fig. 50 — Toboggan

Fig. 51 —Fiberglass pulk. Other models are available for cargo and rescue.

FLASHLIGHTS AND BATTERIES

The ideal all-around battery light for winter use would be waterproof and have a battery capable of high yield at low temperatures. It would be made for use as a low-drain dome light for general illumination and as a high-drain spotlight. It would be operated with the battery case in a pocket and it would be designed for a lamp holder suspended, attached to a wall or to the forehead, or placed upright on a flat surface.

It is possible to make a "D" lithium cell headlight at home. Install the battery in your own type of case to appropriate positive and negative terminals, and connect a good switch. The headlamp proper would be purchased. See Fig. 53.

Some batteries decline substantially in voltage output as the temperature drops (see Table 8). According to Duracell International, battery performance at low temperatures is governed primarily by the amount of drain. At low drain satisfactory performance can be expected, otherwise not. Size of the cell is also important. In other words, use "D" cells and as dim a light as possible.

100 EQUIPMENT

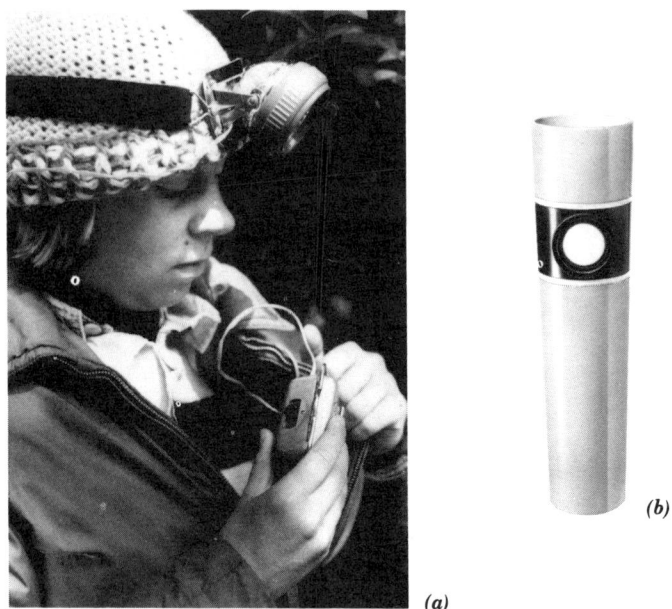

Fig. 52 —(a) Headlight (b) Waterproof, "C" cell flashlight with push-button switch.

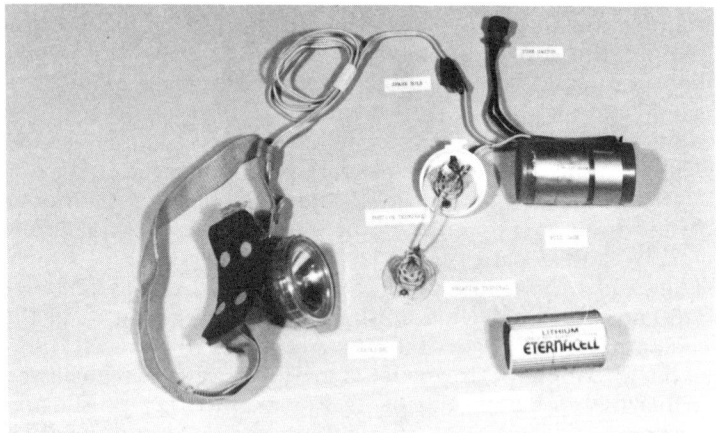

Fig. 53 —Lithium battery powered headlight. Battery fits into pill container between homemade spring terminals, and is controlled by a turn switch.

With respect to mercury oxide batteries used in cameras, Duracell reports that such batteries containing sodium-hydroxide electrolyte are not efficient at all at low temperatures. Those containing potassium-hydroxide electrolyte will operate better. The company also said that silver oxide cells should be better than mercuric oxide types.

Use alkaline (manganese alkaline) or lithium nonrechargeable batteries for maximum low-temperature performance. An alkaline "D" cell weighs about 40% more than the carbon-zinc (4.3 oz. vs. 3.0 oz.), costs almost four times as much, recuperates faster in intermittent use, has a longer shelf life (7 years vs. 4 years), and is less likely to leak when "dead."

The lithium cell weighs 2.9 oz., has 2.8 volts (nominal) vs. 3 volts in 2 alkaline cells, provides about 2½ times more service hours (at 70°F), and furnishes power at much lower temperatures, as indicated in the table. Estimated cost per service hour is about the same. What is most significant is the big weight saving. On the basis of weight and its power at below-zero temperatures, the lithium battery has superior advantages for winter use.

Alkaline rechargeable batteries also retain power at low temperatures. However, initial starting voltage is 1.25 volts, and capacity slowly decreases over service life each time a battery is recharged. According to General Electric Company, service life can be measured by the number of charge-discharge cycles required to reduce capacity to 50% of rated value. This can be 1,000 cycles at 25°C, but usually will have at least 80% of capacity for 500 cycles. Charging time at the overnight rate is 14–16 hours. It appears that rechargeables have limited utility for winter use since they must be recharged before voltage goes below 1.2 volts. If voltage drops down to 0.9 volt, the batteries may be ruined. Unless the batteries are freshly charged and tested with a battery tester, one could start a trip with an unreliable light.

Obtain your batteries from a store that has a high stock turnover, since battery life, especially of the zinc carbon, declines in storage. Be sure to start with a reasonably fresh set.

The choice of bulb affects service life. The usual bulb is the PR-2, with a drain of about 500 milliamperes and a resistance of approximately 5 ohms. Use of a PR-4 or PR-6 bulb with higher resistance makes a drain of about 300 milliamperes. Service life thus is significantly increased by using bulbs with

TABLE 8
Effects of Temperature Changes on "D" Cells[63]
Per Cent of Full Voltage

Temperature, °F	Nickel-Cadmium (recharg.)	Zinc Carbon	Zinc Chloride	Alkaline	Lithium
70	100	100	100	100	100
60	100	90	95	96	100
40	100	69	85	88	100
30	100	59	80	84	100
20	98	48	70	80	100
0	83	27	45	72	100
−20	55	6	10[e]	20	93

e—estimated

higher resistances. Be sure to take along a spare bulb. Reversing one of the batteries in your light before stuffing it in the pack will prevent premature burnout if the switch gets turned on accidentally.

To prevent voltage drop with temperature, the headlight battery should be kept warm in a pocket and the light used only as long as necessary. Most flashlights provide more illumination than necessary around camp, thus wasting energy.

A cheap light will give poor results. A good one will have larger switch contacts made of brass, which is a better conductor at low temperatures. You can improve a light by taking out the steel coil spring in the end and replacing it with one made of spring-tempered brass wire. Clean contacts with steel wool or fine emery cloth. To improve the reliability of your light, solder insulated copper jumper wires between all connections.

If two alkaline batteries and a low-drain bulb are put in the Eveready waterproof flashlight shown in Fig. 52, featuring brass contacts, one would have a reliable hand light for moderate temperatures, in wet weather as well as dry. When placing the light in the pack, avoid putting pressure on the switch.

For a reserve light one could use a folding candle lantern. A carbide lantern will not work if frozen.

CAMERAS AND FILM

For low-temperature work a still camera should have certain characteristics:

1. The film should wind with the emulsion side in.
2. The shutter should be capable of being cocked independently.
3. If the camera is to be used often and for long periods in the cold, it should be "winterized." This includes use of special low-temperature oil and perhaps machining of parts to allow greater clearance. Winterization is expensive, and use of such a camera should be confined to extreme low-temperature conditions. However, note that newer cameras today are lubricated with a broad-range lubricant for better performance at low temperatures.[24]

Minimum camera trouble can be expected if the moving parts are operated for a break-in period prior to use. A camera can be kept warm underneath the parka next to the body. The lens should be inspected for lint attracted from clothing by static electricity. Flash batteries should be kept warm inside the clothing. Note that your camera exposure system may depend on a battery.

In extreme cold, camera operation should be kept as simple as possible. If the camera is not automatic, a handy exposure table can be printed on a card or the camera cover for quick reference. Breathing on the lens should be avoided, since the moisture thus formed will freeze. Avoid touching metal parts with the bare hand. Cover handled metal parts with tape to prevent this, or wear silk or thin cotton gloves.

Consider using a 35 mm camera, without the case, underneath the parka. The camera would be supported by a shoulder harness and held (can be Velcro tape) against the chest for warmth. The lens can be protected by a skylight or ultra violet filter and a lens hood. A camera case makes picture taking more difficult, and good shots can be lost.

Expose your camera to the cold as little as possible so that appreciable condensation will not form on it when it is returned underneath the parka. A photographer's vest with numerous handy pockets can be worn under the parka. A small belt pack, with the bag turned to the front, can also be used for photo items. Some photographers use hand warmers in the storage pockets and a chemical heating pad fastened to the camera. Consider increasing the size of levers and knobs so that the camera can be operated more easily with thick gloves.

Condensation Problems

A cold camera should not be used in a warm room until it has warmed to room temperature. Condensation caused by taking a cold camera into a warm room can be avoided by leaving the camera in a room with a temperature of about 32°F. Another method is to put it in an air-tight rubber or plastic bag before taking it indoors. Then condensation will form on the outside of the bag, not inside on the camera. The camera may be taken outdoors any time, ready for use. But note that if a warm camera is taken outdoors and snow is allowed to fall on it, some of the snow will melt and may later turn to ice.

Shutters

Shutters, especially of the focal-plane type, usually operate slower at low temperatures. A focal-plane shutter made of rubberized fabric may become inoperable because of stiffening. Fast shutter speeds are affected more than slow speeds. Before taking a picture, snap the shutter at 1/10 sec. several times. If the shutter remains cocked for a long period, the chance of freezing in that position increases.

It is possible to get a picture even if the focusing mechanism and diaphragm (but not the shutter mechanism) freeze. Before going out, set the focus and aperture for the conditions expected. Remember that focus on the hyperfocal distance yields the greatest depth of field.

Film

Film gets more brittle as the temperature drops; the leader may break; sprocket holes may tear. Breakage can be avoided by using the film as soon as it is removed from the package; then the cold, dry air will not have time to reduce the moisture content and increase brittleness. Advance film slowly.

The tendency of film to break is less if it is bent around the spool with the emulsion side in — a built-in camera feature. Careful film handling is essential. The type and condition of the camera also may determine whether a film will break or crack. Film should not be left in the camera too long, because of drying. Load film and preset camera indoors whenever possible.

As a rule, high-speed film is not recommended for snow photography, because there is so much light. Superior pictures can be obtained with a medium-speed film such as Kodak Plus-X Pan or Ektachrome, or a slower, fine-grain film such as Panatomic-X or Kodachrome 25. Exposures should be minimal; overexposure is to be avoided. Bracket your exposures ½ stop below and above estimated correct exposure. If both color and black-and-white prints are desired, use Kodacolor or film of a similar type. From the color negative both a black-and-white print and a slide can be made.

EQUIPMENT CHECKLIST

Items for Each Individual

Pack
Sleeping bag (one emergency bag should be carried by party on day hike)
Foam pad; air mattress
Can opener, GI
Cup
Deep plate
Knife and tablespoon
Line, ⅛ in., nylon (for securing tent, pack, etc.)
Line, ¼ in., nylon (for assistance on a pitch, but not for technical climbing)
Leather or neoprene strap with buckle and length of rawhide (emergency snowshoe harness)
Compass
Maps
Watch
Snowshoes, ski poles
Skis, ski poles, skins or climbing wax, ski tip
Ice ax
Crampons, protective bag or spike tips
Creepers (not for climbing)
Camera and film
Signaling mirror
Whistle
Fire-starters or candle
Sunburn ointment
Sunglasses or goggles
Waterproofed "strike anywhere" matches with container

106   EQUIPMENT

First-aid kit
Canteen
Vacuum bottle
Headlight
Hand warmer
Toilet paper
Small insulated pad for sitting on snow
Waterproof refuse bag

Items for Party

Tent with poles, snow stakes, or anchors
Stove with heat resistant board
Extra fuel for stove
Primer fuel for stove
Snow shovel
Pot with bail
Snow bag
Repair kit: combination tool (wrench, plier, screwdriver), flexible wire, needle and thread, tape

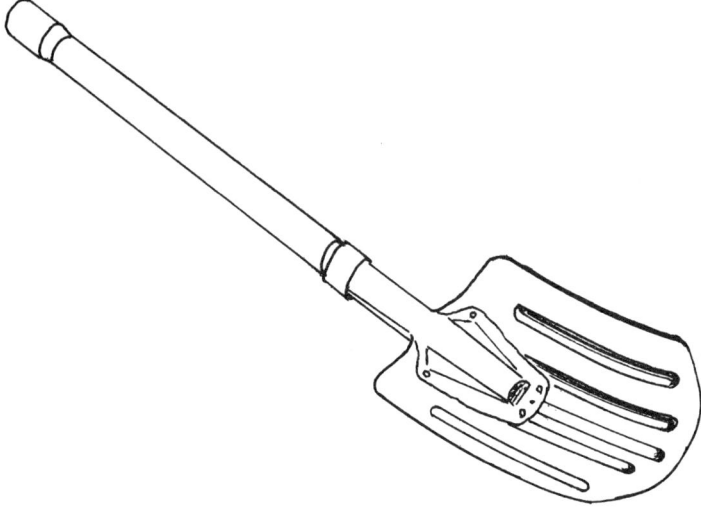

Fig. 54 — Snow shovel with detachable handle.

EQUIPMENT 107

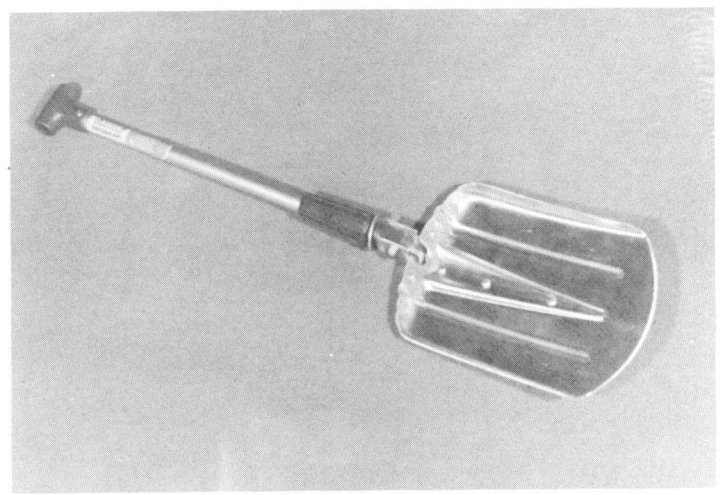

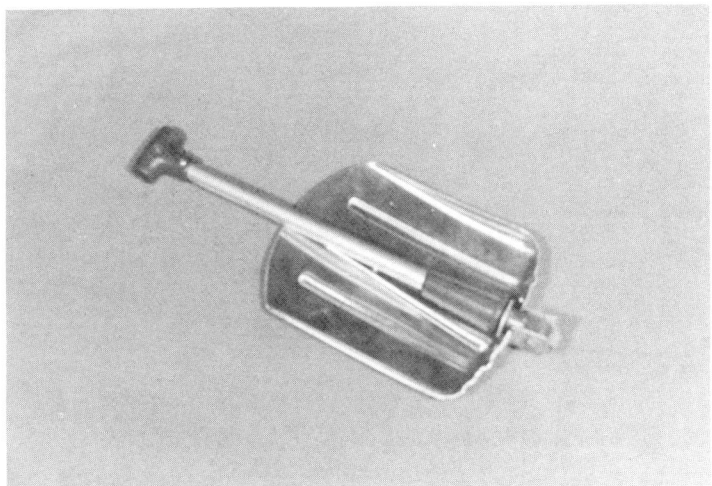

Fig. 55 — Folding snow shovel.

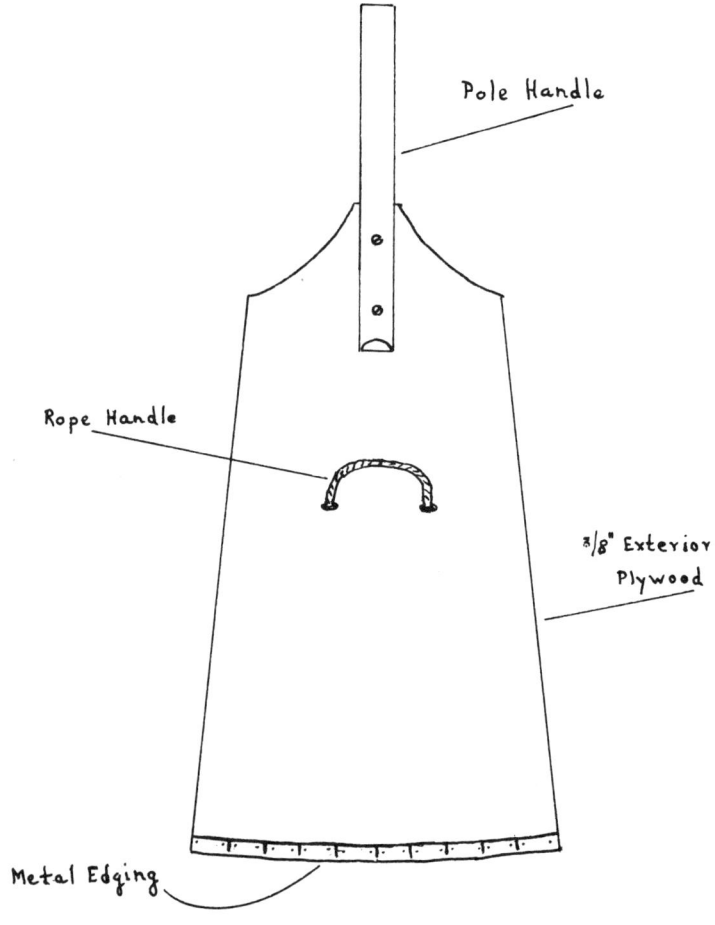

Fig. 56 — Homemade "Eskimo" snow shovel.

Food

IN A COLD CLIMATE food becomes critically important to maintain body temperature, to provide energy for involuntary body functions, and for moving about under varying conditions. Since the early part of World War II, much research and testing have been done to determine how much food is necessary, what kinds, and the value of special supplements.

ENERGY EXPENDITURE

Table 9 gives comparative data on the expenditure of energy in ordinary activities and ordinary walking or mountain climbing. The table indicates that 10 mi. (16 km) of winter hiking in snow with a pack, with 2,000 to 3,000 ft. of climb, could require 5,000 to 6,000 kilogram-calories. These figures are only estimates, but they show that one must be prepared, physically and mentally, for an extremely high energy output in winter climbing.

FOOD REQUIREMENTS

Food is our only source of energy, except for energy stores in the body. The energy expended has to be offset by our net food intake; otherwise the energy deficiency will be borrowed from our tissues, which means loss of weight. For strenuous winter climbing, plan for a daily intake of up to 6,000 kilogram-calories, depending upon the particular conditions encountered—severity of cold, angle of climb, depth of snow, terrain, ice conditions, etc.—not to mention your skill in climbing and whether or not you are a heavy eater. The prudent winter climber chooses his ration carefully for high caloric content, ease of preparation, and low unit weight if it is to be backpacked.

Our diet consists of proteins, carbohydrates, and fats. If you have forgotten their dietary uses, consult some of the books in the Bibliography or a cookbook.

TABLE 9
Energy Expenditure in Various Types of Activities

Activity	Energy Spent per Day[64] (Kilogram-calories)
Basal (lying in bed)	1,500
Sedentary occupation	2,500–3,000
Heavy manual labor	4,000–4,500
Mountain walking (oxygen consumption actually measured en route): 3 miles along roads, 10 miles cross-country, 2,550 feet climbed	4,110 (day total)

	Energy Spent per Min. (Kilogram-calories)
Hiking barefoot on hard snow—3.6 mph	11.9
Hiking barefoot on loose snow with 44 lb. load—2.4 mph	20.2
Hiking with snowshoes on loose snow—2.4 mph	13.8
Skiing level on hard snow—3.6 mph	9.9

At least half of the protein should be of high value, such as meat, milk and cheese. Vitamins, minerals and bulk come from proteins, fats and carbohydrates.

Foods of high fat and protein content are particularly desirable in the morning and evening. Extra fat can easily be supplied by adding a little extra butter or margarine to soups, cereal, tea, etc. Although fat is a rich source of energy, one does not have to plan a daily ration for high fat content. In studies made by the U.S. Army there was no indication of "fat hunger" due to cold[35]. It is not essential to include *large* amounts of butter and other fat items.

One-day Trip

Any lunch that you have ordinarily will probably suffice. Take along foods you like. Special foods for a short trip are usually not necessary, but consideration should be given to the following advice.

Food carried should be of the easily digestible, high-energy type. It should be handy for nibbling—hard candies, dried fruit, fresh fruit (if it can be prevented from freezing), nuts, fruit cake, cheese, hard-boiled eggs. Cheese and hard-boiled eggs spoil on thawing after freezing, so insulate them. Carry a full vacuum bottle of hot coffee, tea, chocolate, or cocoa, gelatin, soup, or even sugared water. Chocolate will sour if not used soon enough. Besides their nutritional and warming value, hot drinks are psychological boosters.

Extended Trip

For a winter backpack trip of more than a day, food planning demands more serious study. Meals should be well prepared, delicious, and plentiful. Meals can and should be tried out in the backyard—or in the kitchen at least—before a winter trip. Aside from comfort and morale, an adequate diet is of critical importance in preventing hypothermia or frostbite.

Simplicity in food preparation is essential. Meals should be of the one-pot variety—called by such romantic names as glop, mulligan, or hoosh — to be simply and speedily heated or cooked on your stove. Basic ingredients are soup mix, vegetables, rice or potatoes, some kind of meat (put in fish if you don't like meat), and seasoning. There are as many varieties as there are amateur cooks. The mixing of different foods in a pot may sound repelling to the sensitive gourmet, but it can result in a concoction that is tasty and appetizing as well as nutritious. Glop presents a grand opportunity for an inventive genius to find by experiment a distinctive and interesting combination.

Your utensils should consist of no more than a tablespoon and a large cup with a non-conducting handle. An insulated cup is preferred by many. Anyone who puts a hot meal from a pot into a big, cold metal plate should see a psychiatrist. And don't bother to wash your cup for the next course — everything gets mixed up eventually—so just scrape out your container. One hiker uses quart size plastic ice cream containers for all his food and beverages. Consider using a waterproof bag for carrying snow into the tent. This would be your handy water supply.

TABLE 10

Energy Values and Recommended Percentages of a Cold-Weather Diet[33]

	Proportion	Kilogram—Calories	
		Per Gram	Per Pound
Protein	40%	4	1,800
Fat	40	9	4,100
Carbohydrates	20	4	1,800

At the end of an exhausting day's hike it is important to be able to get a meal with minimum effort, perhaps while resting and keeping warm inside a tent and in one's sleeping bag. Consider foods that can be eaten cold if the circumstances require it; some hikers take extra lunch and nibbling items for this purpose.

Dehydrated, main-course foods are generally not suited for winter camping on account of the need for rehydration, longer preparation, and longer cooking. Yet some winter climbers prefer them. On an extended trip, where you are completely dependent on your own supply, the lightness of dehydrated food more than offsets the disadvantages.

Freeze-dried foods fit nicely into winter camping needs. A meal is quickly and easily prepared just by adding boiling water, so less fuel is necessary. Although the monetary cost is greater, it is not prohibitive from a recreational point of view. It is not necessary to pay fancy prices for freeze-dried or dehydrated foods at outdoor supply stores. Your local supermarket or grocery has many substitute items at much lower cost.

Store price is not the only price one pays—that is, society pays. *Environmental cost must be added.*

All kinds of disposable packaging and containers inflict their visible pollution and hidden costs everywhere — in the city, suburbs, rural areas; on streets, at the stadium, in parks; on trails, at shelters and campsites. The result is not only increased governmental cost on account of cleanup by paid sanitation crews and incineration and dumping at landfills, but also increased fire hazards, injury or damage by broken glass, ground water pollution, and probably a whole list of other effects. Heavy expenditure of volunteer time and effort in collecting trail litter in a massive Annual Cleanup Day, like that of the NY/NJ Trail Conference, is also mandatory. The cleanup statistics from this effort—bags of litter, etc.—are staggering.

Make your own assessment of the environmental cost and consider what you must do to reduce it.

One has to be careful in selecting freeze-dried foods, especially dinners. Instead of having a satisfying meal, you could have a disaster—a mess not associated with anything seen or tasted before, having to eat any spare food you have and probably still going hungry. Still on the negative side, one hiker's comments:

"Non-rehydrated pieces of meat and vegetables were found and these had the consistency of chalk and tasted like spiced plastic. Longer rehydration time and more stirring failed to alleviate the problem.

"All the entrees were pitifully small. On one recent trip three of us ate two two-man dinners at each meal and still found it necessary to supplement the portions with bread and cakes.

"Most of the entrees leave an aftertaste, perhaps from chemicals used in their preparation."

Another comment—not by a hiker—summed up:

When compared to fresh food and frozen food, freeze-dried comes in a poor second.

A thorough study and evaluation of freeze-dried dinners was conducted by *Backpacker* magazine[7], including valuable tips on supermarket substitutes. This study would be most helpful in selecting the best dinner.

Summary finding: "After extensive tests of all the available lightweight food dinners, we found—somewhat to our surprise—that freeze-dried dinners are pretty good." Ratings were made on the basis of cost, weight, ease of opening package, backpackability, ease of preparation (including clarity of directions), amount of water required, cooking time, appearance, smell, taste, fillingness, ease of cleanup, and environmental consciousness as evidenced in the packaging or company literature.

The winter camper should pay particular attention to the amount of water needed, whether or not cooking is necessary (as opposed to adding boiling water), fillingness (reduce "number fed" in half), and nutritional value (consider adding fat or other supplements).

Many hikers have their meals while in their sleeping bags, or get into their sacks right after a meal. If considerable time elapses between the meal and getting into the sack for the night, eat a snack, either as a supplement to the day's ration or as part of it. The snack will produce enough heat in the body during the night to assure 1 to 1½ hours of additional sleep. Without this supplement a person may be awakened by the cold. This has been proved in controlled tests at $-30°F$.

Vitamin C tablets can supplement natural sources, although neither this vitamin nor any other will increase one's resistance to cold.

Dehydration in winter climbing is considerable unless adequate liquids are consumed. Dehydration hastens the onset of general fatigue and enhances the probability of constipation. Eating snow for a short period is harmless; if done to excess it can cause the mucous lining of the mouth to become inflamed and painful. If you need to get water from snow, fill a waterproof bag, secure the opening, then place the bag next to your body under your parka. Experience will tell you how long to wait for melting. To prevent freezing of a canteen cap, stow your canteen of water upside down and inside your pack.

Palatable hot drinks should be available in quantity in the morning and evening. Sufficient liquids—at least 2 qts.—should be provided each day to compensate for loss through sweating, breathing, and elimination. Salt, which helps retention of body water, can come from such sources as peanuts, food seasonings, or salt tablets. Low salt intake can be a subtle crippler on long trips.

Certain foods, such as quick-cooking oats, can be cooked in comination with snow or ice. Add butter or margarine.

CHECKLIST OF SUITABLE FOODS

Proteins:

Dehydrated eggs (including ham, cheese mixes)
Hard-boiled eggs (insulate)
Beef jerky, meat bar, precooked sausage, salami, bologna, chipped beef, pepperoni, Canadian bacon
Canned meats—roast beef, chicken or turkey, corned beef, meat balls, hamburger
Canned sardines, tuna fish
Cheese, natural or process (insulate)
Nuts, salted

Carbohydrates:

Oatmeal or other cereals
Soup mixes
Dehydrated potatoes, powder or flakes
Instant rice
Hardtack or other durable biscuit
Vegetables, dehydrated or freeze-dried
Fruit cake
Sugar, white or brown
Fruit bars, cookies (home-baked)

Dried fruit—raisins, dates, apricots, peaches
Mincemeat
Instant pudding mixes
Candy bars, gum drops

Fats:

Butter or margarine

Beverages:

Powdered chocolate or cocoa, lemonade, orangeade, etc.
Powdered whole milk
Fortified beverage (instant breakfasts, etc.)
Tea, bouillon
Fruit gelatine

Delicacies:

Crabmeat, canned
Shrimp, canned
Cocktail sausages

Flavoring:

Salt, pepper
Onion flakes
Tomato flakes

SUGGESTED MENU FOR A ONE-WEEK TRIP

Breakfast

Cereal
Prepackaged oatmeal, raisins, wheat germ, nuts, brown sugar. Substitute other nourishing cereal for variety.
Fruit
Pitted prunes. Substitute apricots or other dried fruit.
Biscuit
Hardtack with butter or margarine and salami. Substitute precooked bacon, ham, jam or peanut butter.
Beverage
Hot tea in vacuum bottle. Substitute cocoa (somewhat diuretic), hot milk, hot fruit gelatin or soup.

Trail Snack

Packaged lunch of sandwiches, etc. and hot beverage in vacuum bottle. Substitute and supplement with gorp; hardtack with peanut butter, jam or sardines; cookies, hard candy, chocolate, dried fruit; hot beverage or water.

Dinner

Soup
   Powdered soup—also used for one-pot glop.
One-pot glop
   Soup; dry milk (to enrich and thicken soup); rice; freeze-dried vegetables (also try frozen); precooked hamburger; salt and pepper; onion flakes or other flavoring. Substitute freeze-dried macaroni, noodles, spaghetti (with cheese or tomatoes), chipped beef, tuna fish, salmon, chicken, salami, meat bar.
Biscuit
   Hardtack with butter or margarine.
Dessert
   Fruit cake. Substitute mincemeat, cookies, dried fruit.
Beverage
   Tea or more soup. Substitute cocoa, fruit gelatin, milk.

The first item would be for the first day of the trip; during the remaining days there will be lots of repetition. It is not prudent to plan for too much variety, but do include some of your favorite delicacies to make the week more gastronomically interesting. Plan your glop to require no more than 15 minutes to prepare.

A picnic on top of Phelps.

Travel

IN WOODED AREAS of the Northeast the ground is quite likely to be covered with snow during most of winter and into spring. When planning an excursion keep in mind that snow depth is likely to increase considerably as woods become thicker and elevation increases — though windswept summits may be bare. Thus at a time when the Hudson Highlands have only a few inches of snow on the ground, the Catskills may have a few feet.

Ordinary hiking on hard-packed snow or in powdery snow up to about 10 in. deep is not very difficult. In powdery snow deeper than this, and in soft wet snow that may be not so deep, snowshoes or skis are likely to be needed. These may be required also if the snow has a crust that one keeps breaking through with ordinary footwear. On an icy surface crampons will be necessary.

Some hikers make the mistake of not taking their snowshoes, because they assume there will be no snow on the trail. At least put them in your car when you leave for the hike. At the start of the hike lash the snowshoes to your pack if there is any chance of encountering deep snow. This precaution is particularly applicable in early spring.

The mechanics of hiking and climbing on snowshoes are simple. "Duck walking" is unnecessary. Start with a natural stance, feet about 12 in. apart, side by side. Move the left foot forward in natural stride, plant it, then lift the rear snowshoe ahead of the other. In this second motion, the inner edge of the right shoe will pass over the inner edge of the other. Interference is further avoided by a beavertail or by a taper toward the rear. As the foot is lifted for each step, the tail of the snowshoe drops as it swivels on the binding. This prevents the toe from digging into the snow and the tail from flipping snow onto one's backside.

You can even run on snowshoes. Try it on an easy, level surface.

On steep pitches in deep snow, climb by kicking steps with the toes. Kick with the same motion you would use when pedaling a bicycle. Keep in balance. Don't bend over the slope, but stand as upright as possible to keep most of your weight over your snowshoes. As you bring your foot up behind for

118 TRAVEL

Snowshoers ascend a slope in the Mahoosucs.

Fig. 57 — Kicking steps with snowshoes.

another step, flick the tail of the snowshoe up so that when your foot starts down, the toe will be horizontal or pointing slightly downward. Use your ski poles too; drive them firmly into the snow below and push upward. If climbing with snowshoes gets too difficult, it may be easier to climb without them by kicking steps with one's boots.

Descent can be speeded by glissading on the seat of the pants for short distances. If your snowshoes have turned-up toes, you can glissade on the snowshoes. Put the toe of the rear snowshoe on the rear of the front snowshoe, weight on heels; crouch, and go. But be sure you can throw your rump in the snow in time to stop. For braking, use the ice ax or ski poles.

CARRYING AND HOLDING AN ICE AX

Learn how to carry the ax properly to minimize the chance of injury to yourself or your trailmates. On easy trails it should be carried by holding it at the balance point on the shaft with the

Fig. 58 —Glissading is a quick way of getting down a steep slope.

spike pointing forward and the pick facing downward. If the spike is pointed rearward, the man behind could run into it accidentally. In case of a fall, the pick will not impale the owner. The ax can also be carried as a cane, grasped at the head with the pick aimed forward. If you don't want to carry it, secure it outside your pack or frame pack with the spike pointed down, so that it does not snag on branches overhead. Most packs, however, are made to carry the shaft upward. Put tape around the head of your ice ax so that it can be held barehanded.

On steep slopes where a fall is possible, be prepared for self-arrest by having your ax in the ready position. Grasp the head with the thumb on the adze side; the other hand holds the shaft near the point and opposite the hip (Fig. 59).

SKI TOURING AND MOUNTAINEERING

Ski touring, unlike ski mountaineering, is for the valleys, where slopes can be climbed with wax and the downhill sections can be skied "wide open." With good technique and a fast surface, the ski tourer can ski 20 or even 30 miles in a day.

Fig. 59 —*Carrying and holding the ice ax.*

Mountain skiing offers a rapid traverse of the approach trail and the opportunity to ski the lower reaches of the mountain and then out on the packed-down approach trail to the car. Being generally downhill, the return may afford a delightful combination of sliding and striding. But ski mountaineering, with the chance to traverse and descend vast, open snowfields

Adirondack touring on a fire truck road.

with sweeping, linked turns, is more a Western phenomenon. In the Northeast, the trails and summits do not lend themselves to this variety of sport. On the approach to timberline, slopes become steep, growth thickens to impede progress, the trail is either narrow and confining or is lost altogether, the wind may be at gale or hurricane force, the temperature may be far down, and the surface may be icy or crusty. Summits are frequently wooded or have limited reaches above timberline. Locations where ski mountaineering may be practiced are comparatively few, examples being the cones of Mt. Marcy and Mt. Washington, the Gulf of Slides Trail and the Sherburne Trail (both on Washington) and some trails on Mansfield. This chapter will describe special ski techniques for climbing and descending under Northeast trail conditions. Refer also to books on ski touring cited in the Bibliography, especially by Lederer and Wilson.[43]

Features of a Planned Ski Touring Trail

Fig. 60 shows features of a planned ski touring trail.

Waxes

Modern touring ski waxes are so improved that many trails can be climbed on wax alone without climbers to about a 14-degree maximum slope. Climbers may still be needed to snub speed on the descent. A somewhat softer or stickier grade of wax will give greater climbing efficiency than is normally recommended for a particular snow condition.

Fiberglass skis with polyethylene bases do not require a base preparation; the running wax can be applied directly to the base. However, some advise putting on an extra hard running wax as a base, or the addition of a binder wax, such as Grundvax, for better running wax adhesion. Both these bases would be rubbed on, then smoothed out with a "cork," perhaps after heating with a torch or iron.

Wood skis require tar compound application to the base to protect the skis from moisture and to be able to put on the running wax. Synthetic tar preparations, such as Grundvalla, come in spray, paint-on or warm-in compounds. Easiest to apply are the two former air-dry types, which may need as much as 12 hours to dry.

124 TRAVEL

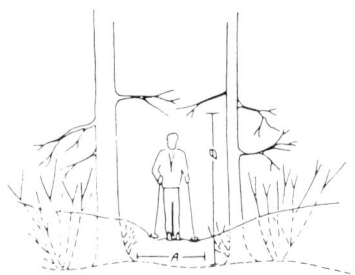

Cross-Section of trail. A: minimum width, 4 feet for one-way trail, 6 feet for two-way trail. B: clear branches to a height of 7 feet plus expected maximum snow depth.

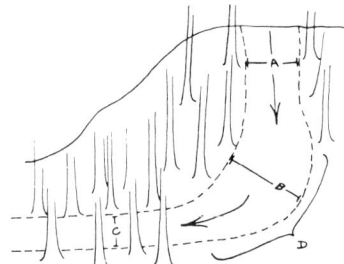

Downhill portion of trail with turn. A: 7-8 feet wide to permit snowplow position. B: turn widened to allow room for snowplow or step turn. C: Gentle slope, only slightly wider than trail on level. D: clear of obstructions in case skier misses turn.

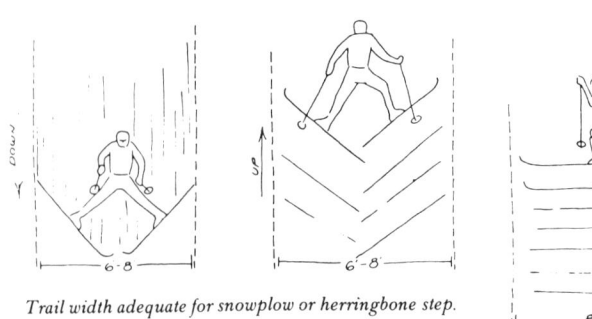

Trail width adequate for snowplow or herringbone step. Slopes, 8-30%. Surface must also be reasonably flat.

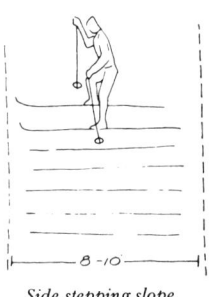

Side stepping slope.

Fig. 60 — Planned features of a ski touring trail.[39]

Skiers of the "old school" are reported to use pine tar, obtainable from a chemical supply house, rather than the commercial preparation.

Warm-in tar compound is first applied with a brush to the ski bottom after removing prior waxes with a scraper and torch or solvent. Wipe off excess wax softened by the torch or solvent. Then with a propane or butane torch (specially designed butane torches are available) in one hand and a rag in the other,

Mt. Van Hoevenberg Trail (Adirondacks)

heat a short section of the ski bottom until the tar starts to boil. Immediately after boiling starts, quickly wipe the tar to a smooth finish. Continue this procedure along the length of the ski and repeat if necessary.

It is possible for a warmed-in base to last the entire season, much longer than the spray-on and paint-on preparations. The latter two methods can be useful for touch up purposes. One should be reminded that a torch has to be used carefully to avoid burning the bottom of the ski. It is best to have skis clamped securely to a bench or pair of "horses" when heating and wiping. "Horses" specially made for tarring and waxing are available. Apply the warm-in base tar to your wood skis at home before leaving, as the lodge or other facility may not allow the use of torches inside. Doing the job outside would probably not be feasible or convenient either.

The following general running wax procedures are substantially common to all brands. Of course consult the waxing instructions for your particular set of waxes. Many skiers will acquire their individual waxing preferences and techniques.

1. Go outside and estimate the temperature and type of snow — new, corn, rough corn, or crust. If temperature is above freezing, also make an estimate of the moisture content. Take a handful of snow and make a snowball. If snow is moist, you can make a ball; wet snow will have a distinct wet surface.
2. Now refer to Table 11, Waxing Guide for Swix Waxes, and estimate wax to use. Of course this estimate has to be checked against actual experience after going about 300 yards. Whenever possible, waxing should be done at room temperature (indoors) on dry skis:
    - Apply wax as evenly as possible over the entire running surface — but not in the groove — in preparation for smoothing. Rub paraffin in the groove. (To keep snow off top of skis, boot heels and pole baskets, apply paraffin on these too.)
    - Rub the ski surface with the heel of your hand or with a "cork" (expanded styrofoam) in any direction until smooth. Wax can also be smoothed with a torch or waxing iron.
    - Add one or two additional wax layers, especially when the tour will be long or over old (corn) snow.

TABLE 11

Waxing Guide for Swix Waxes

Temperature/Moisture	Type of snow			Use
	New	Old (Corn)	Rough Corn Snow, Crust & Ice	
18°F and below	x			Special green wax
10°F and below		x		Special green wax
18°F to 27°F	x			Green wax
10°F to 21°F		x		Green wax
27°F to 32°F	x			Blue wax
21°F to 30°F		x		Blue wax
Below freezing			x	Blue klister
Freezing to thawing, 32°F	x	x		Violet wax
Crust and wet snow, 25°F to 37°F			x	Violet klister
Soggy snow, slipping tracks	x			Red wax
Soggy snow		x		Red wax
Wet or soaking wet snow		x	x	Red klister
Wet snow	x			Yellow klister

Notes—

Kinds of snow: New snow—sharp-edged snowflake crystals (fine-grain snow); old (corn) snow—rounded or angular grains without typical crystals; crusted snow—snow frozen together in a layer.

Types of waxes: Hard waxes—come in round cans, used for temperatures below freezing; klister waxes—tacky-hard waxes in round cans, used for temperatures around freezing; klisters—tacky fluids in tubes, used for temperatures slightly below and above freezing, and for ice and crust.

Tip: To facilitate remembering hardness order, mark can at bottom with your own number or letter system.

- If in doubt about wax to use, start with a hard, low temperature wax. If this does not grip, stop and apply a layer of the next softer wax. *If you first apply a wax that is too soft, snow will strongly adhere to the ski and you cannot ski at all. The wax must be removed and the ski rewaxed.*

3. If both dry and wet snow may be encountered, at the start you can try a soft wax application to the middle third of your skis (foot). If that does not grip, apply that wax over the entire ski. The thickness of the additional applications depends on the temperature. If that wax does not allow you to climb, add a klister to the foot of the ski. When in doubt as to thickness, apply a thin layer. Smooth with a flat stick or with the scraper of the cork-scraper tool. (Whenever possible klister waxes should be applied at room temperature to

128   TRAVEL

Fig. 61—Step turn: A most useful forest skiing maneuver. Quickly set one ski in the new direction of travel, then bring the other ski quickly alongside.

Fig. 62—Skiing stride: Move ski forward in a long stride so that tip of rear ski is even with forward foot. As stride wanes, lift the rear ski slightly and quickly stride forward. Note how the rear foot bends to allow the ski tip to hang down and follow the track.

get it smooth. Smoothest klister is made by first heating with a torch, then spreading with a paint brush. Be sure to keep klister out of grooves and off the sides of skis.)
4. A good method to follow if you do not have the waxing table or if you do not want to refer to a table, is to start with a hard wax. Then use the principle explained above for dry-wet

conditions, that is progressively add softer waxes beginning with a layer on the foot of the ski.

Waxing can be frustrating. Snow conditions vary — in the woods vs. open slope, sunny slopes vs. shady slopes, packed trail vs. unpacked off trail, etc. So please don't think waxing is going to be easy. It's an art; you have to learn by experience. Remember that soft wax has to be removed before applying a harder wax. If waxes cause too much trouble, rewax with paraffin or a downhill wax and use side stepping, herringbone and variations to climb.

Wide-range wax kits are now on the market featuring just two grades of wax, a hard wax for dry powder snow and a soft wax for wet snow. To get this versatility some speed is sac-

TABLE 12

Waxing Chart for Wide-Range Waxes

TEMPERATURE	WAX APPLIED	WAX TYPES			
		Johannsen Jack Rabbit	Ostbye Duo	Swix Starter	Toko Touring
40°	ROUGH	Wet	Yellow	Plus	Silver
32°	SMOOTH				
	ROUGH				
	SMOOTH	Dry	Blue	Minus	Gold
20°	POLISHED				
16°					

130 TRAVEL

Fig. 63 — Climbing methods.

rificed. By first applying the hard wax in layers and gradually progressing with overlayers of soft wax, one finds the point at which the skis will grip under existing snow conditions.

In climbing with wax, stamp the ski forward, stepping firmly on the snow while shifting your entire weight to that ski without allowing any backslip. This action allows interlocking sharp edges and points of snow crystals time to adhere to the wax surface. As you accumulate skiing experience, your climbing skill will improve; you will speedily and easily go up the grades.

When the slope gets steeper and backslip occurs more often, it is time to shift to climbers.

Climbers

The modern technique is to use one of three types of "skins": sealskin, plush strip, or nylon-mohair strip. The latter is secured to the ski, even over wax, by the adhesive backing on the strip, whereas sealskin and plush are fastened with straps and clips. Rearward pointing nap on these skins give both grip and glide. When going downhill, sliding speed is snubbed to an even, relaxed pace — about one-half normal — thus giving a measure of speed control.

Fig. 64 — Bag-type climber: Bag is longer than ski. It wrinkles while going up, trails out flat while going down. While going down, front end of bag does not always stay in contact with ski but acts as a scoop, placing great strain on the attachment. Bag climbers were popular before advent of good touring waxes and are only slightly more effective.

Fig. 65 — Mesh climber: Rear pocket.

When stopping to put on skins, stamp down a patch of snow. Then lay the ski poles on the packed snow parallel and at right angles to the remaining ski, handles resting in front of the boot, baskets lying more or less flat. This arrangement will provide good support for the free foot with no damage to the poles.

Skins must be tightly secured. Any slack that develops will cause the skin to work off the ski tip going uphill, loosen from the tail going downhill, or be pulled off when side-slipping.

Practice putting skins on at home, preferably with mittens, so that the job can be done expeditiously on the trail. You should have a special bag or available side pocket for the skins so that when you remove them they will not wet other items in your pack.

One should know about other types of climbers as well: the bag-type, mesh, and rope. The first is a loose canvas bag slipped over the tail of the ski and fastened with a strap in front of the foot. In climbing and as the ski slips back, the bag wrinkles, thus gripping. When sliding forward, the bag smooths out. The bag can be used up to about a 14-degree grade, about the same as wax. Mesh is a strip of tough nylon with a front strap and rear pocket. With mesh the ski will not slide, but it is light and will allow climbing a slightly steeper grade—about 22 degrees—than with skins. By rope is meant a ¼″ line spiraled around the ski to form a diamond pattern. This climber is easily made at home at low cost and makes a most efficient and reliable climber—to a maximum grade of about 25 degrees—but will not slide. One has to walk the skis, but rope can provide added safety on crusty or icy slopes when descending. Rope will stay in place on the ski under almost any condition.

To make rope climbers use ¼-inch rope three times the length of your ski. Refer to Fig. 66. Make a small loop on rope center, place loop over tip, and spiral both ends down ski. Determine cross-over points. At cross-over point (1) raise a strand and make an opening through which to pass the rope. Repeat this step in the opposite direction to form a diamond (2–3). Slip climber (with four diamonds: one behind foot, one under foot, and two between foot and tip) over ski (4), and place small loop over ski tip. Rope in the right hand will pass around the tail, to be secured as shown in Fig. 67. Install S-hook, wood slider, and small clamp on the tail rope. Connect the S-hook at the first cross-over point on top of the ski. Tighten and secure by slipping the clamp over the slider.

Should a person suffer a minor injury such that he can walk but not ski, cord can be wrapped about the skis to act as a snubber, enabling the injured person to walk out slowly.

Pole-Braking

Poles for climbing should have large baskets for soft, deep snow. If your poles have small baskets, you can attach basket extenders. A large basket gives greater support than a small basket going uphill and more drag going down. For hard-crust snow, ski pole points must cut into the crust to give any braking effect. Hands should not be put through the loops, since a basket may snag on a branch or stump. Also, you want to be able to shift the hands quickly down on the shafts in case of a fall.

On short downhill stretches where the slope is too steep for simple snowplow control and not long enough or steep enough to use climbers, pole-braking is recommended.

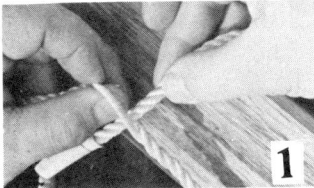   

Fig. 66 — Making Rope Climbers

Pole-braking methods include the double-hand brake, the thigh-seat brake and the side brake.

The double-hand brake is done in a crouching position with poles outside the skis next to your boots, held near the basket, thumbs forward, with the upper part of the pole behind the arm and pressed against the armpit. Increasing the pressure of the points on the snow increases the braking action.

The thigh-seat brake also can be done in a crouching position. Both poles are held together under the right thigh, baskets to the rear. The right hand grasps the poles just above the

134 TRAVEL

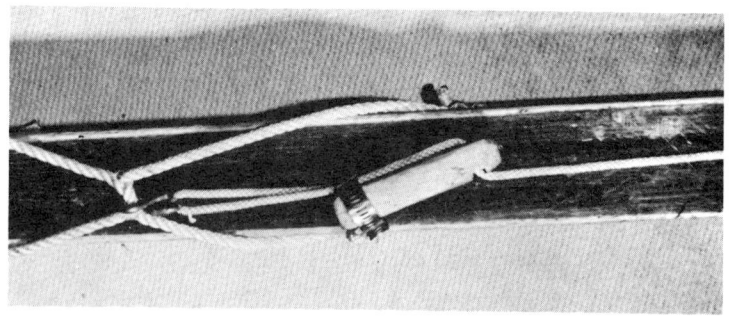

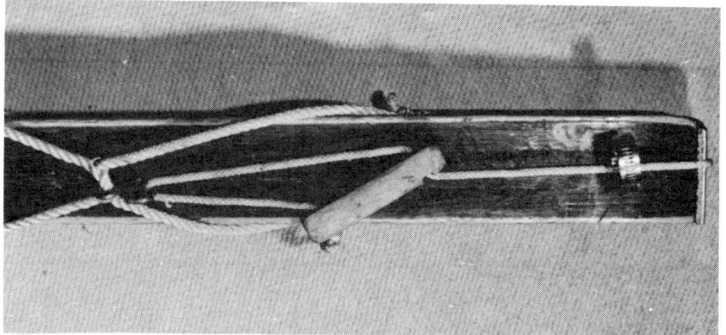

Fig. 67—Securing the Rope Climber

baskets, the upper part resting in the left arm at the elbow. Considerable leverage is thus applied to the baskets as they drag in the snow. Care must be taken to avoid breaking the poles.

Side braking is done by holding both poles together in a semi-crouching position, one hand low down on the poles, the other up high so that leverage can be applied to the dragging baskets. Short turns or a full stop can be made by using the pole as a pivot point and the outside ski in the stem position. This is very effective when wearing a pack.

At times skins may be needed on the descent as well as in climbing. Skis should be placed flat and straight ahead, not angled.

A falling stop may be unprofessional and undignified, but when other methods fail, it is preferable to crashing into a grove of trees or a gully.

Fig. 68 — Pole-braking.

If you manage to remain upright, the telemark — one ski ahead of the other and about 7 inches apart, body in a crouched position — will improve forward stability on rough terrain or fast runs into deep snow.

Equipment Failures

Any equipment failure in a remote area can be serious. Note these problems:

1. *Heel cables slipping off the boot heel:* Have cord available to tie over the instep.
2. *Screws loosening with cable bindings:* Interlocking teeth lose contact and the binding spreads open. Tighten screws. Insert a tiny twig in the screw hole to get a better bite.
3. *Heel cable breaking or stretching:* Use a spare heel cable or make cord cable (Fig. 70).
4. *Baskets coming off ski poles:* Usually the cotter pin that holds the basket in place goes too. Resecure the basket with wire.
5. *Broken or lost binding bail:* Carry a spare of the type you use. Reminder: The emergency repair kit should include a combination tool, cord, soft wire, screws, and hose clamp or

136 TRAVEL

Fig. 69—Telemark for run out on rough trail.

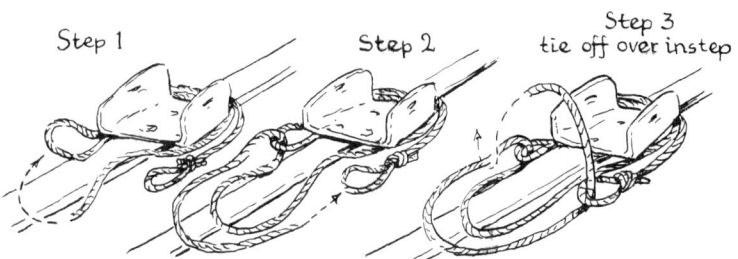

Fig. 70—Making emergency heel cable with cord.

tape. Also carry a clamp-on ski tip. If your tip breaks and you don't have a clamp-on tip, an emergency repair can be made as illustrated in Fig. 71.

Fig. 72 shows a combination tool made at home at less cost than a purchased one. The unit is made from two separate tools, an adjustable plier and a 6-inch adjustable wrench. Cut off about 2 inches of handle on the plier and about 1 inch of the wrench handle. Then braze or electric weld the wrench handle to the shortened plier handle. Grind a screwdriver tip on the other plier handle. A local welder may do the job for a nominal amount or as a goodwill gesture.

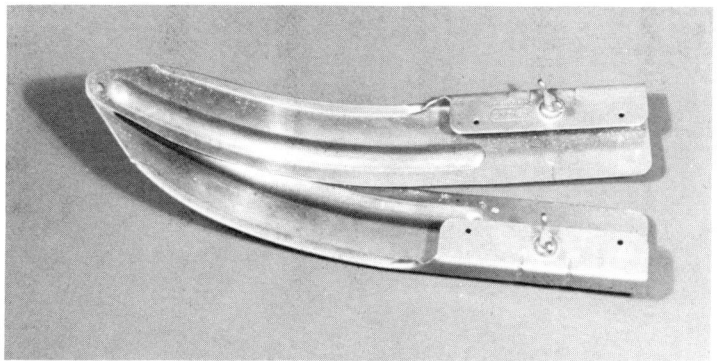

Fig. 71—Clamp-on ski tip.

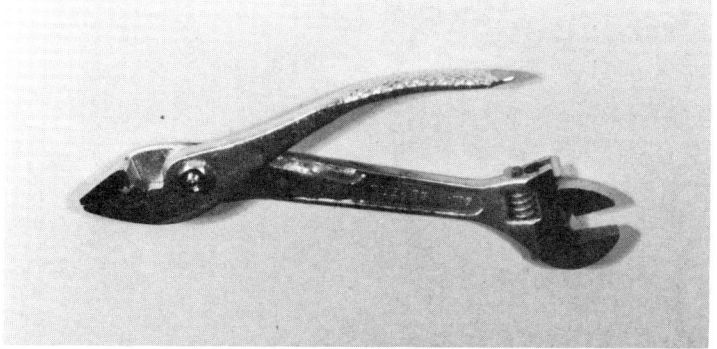

Fig. 72—Homemade combination tool.

138 TRAVEL

To make an emergency repair of a broken wood ski tip, refer to Fig. 73:

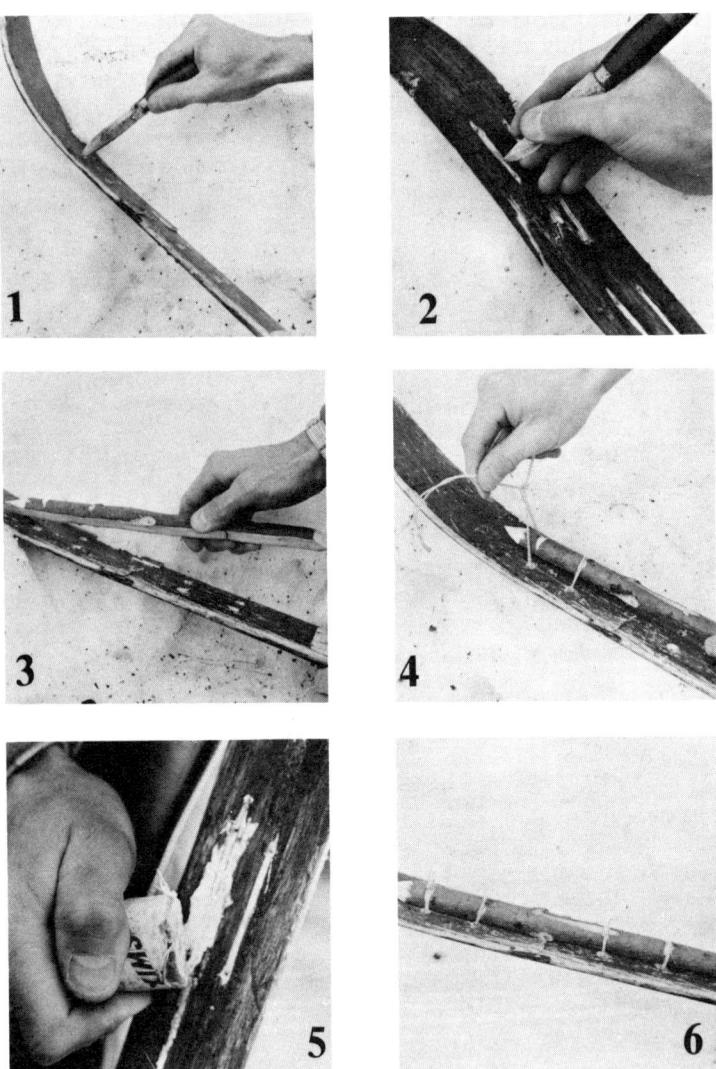

Fig. 73—Field repair of broken ski tip.

1. Drill a rectangular pattern of four holes on each side of the break.
2. On the bottom and on each side of the break carve a groove between the holes, deep enough for lashing cord or wire to be below the running surface.
3. Get a stout stick longer than the distance between the holes. Point the ends and trim the side of the stick that will lie against the top of the ski. Notch the top in four places to match holes.
4. Run cord or wire down through the holes on each side of notch, along the bottom and up through the next pair of holes, and secure on top. Repeat on the other side of the break.
5. Rub ski wax heavily on the cord or wire on the bottom to hold it in place and protect it from wear.
6. The finished repair job.

Trail Courtesy for Skiers

- Always fill in sitzmarks. Keep the track smooth for the next skiers.
- Never walk on ski trails. If you remove your skis, walk on the side.
- Yield to skiers coming downhill. If you must stop, move over to one side to allow fast skiers to pass. Watch out for snowshoers on hiking trails.
- If about to pass a skier on the trail, yell "track."
- Travel in the preferred direction when specified.

CROSSING ICE

Winter hiking may involve crossing ice on streams, lakes, or swamps. It is vital for the hiker to know something about safety on ice and what to do when someone breaks through. Probable survival time in 32°F water is about 20 minutes. In a particular winter situation it may actually be considerably less.

Sometimes slush may underly a blanket of snow. In addition to the resistance caused by the slush, it may quickly freeze to the skis.

Characteristics of Ice

Clear ice 2 in. thick will support one person on foot; 3 in. will support a group in single file. For slush ice frozen hard, double these thicknesses — and be sure that the slush is frozen to sufficient depth. Skis and snowshoes spread weight and thus reduce the likelihood of breaking through. If one has to stand "barefoot" on risky ice, spread the legs apart as far as they will comfortably go.

The strength of ice varies from place to place. The water may be warmer and the ice thinner in shallows and near springs. Ice often is thinner at inlets and outlets of ponds because of the water's motion. Ice on streams usually is thinner where the flow is faster. Where the water level has fallen since the ice formed, the ice is no longer supported by the water and thus may break relatively easily under a hiker's weight. Ice in swamps tends to be relatively weak in shallows and in masses of grass or other vegetation. Wherever ice is covered with snow, it should be suspect.

On quiet water, 2 or 3 in. of ice can form during one night of temperatures near zero. But one day of temperatures above freezing can thin the ice considerably, especially near shore. It is unsafe to estimate the thickness of ice purely on the basis of present or recent weather. And this is especially true if the ice is covered with snow, because of the snow's insulating effect. In general it is wise not to venture out on ice if there is any doubt at all as to its strength. Never go on untested ice while alone.

Rescue of a Hiker Who Has Broken Through

If a person breaks through ice in deep water, quick action is needed. The party immediately spreads out. A rope with a noose should be thrown to the victim to put around his waist so that he can be pulled out or supported while other rescue action is taken. Since ice around the hole is likely to break if the victim tries to climb onto it, the hole should be spanned with skis, a sapling, or branches. One or two rescuers — not more than the ice can hold — should use skis, snowshoes, or branches to spread their weight on the ice while they pull the victim out. An alternative method is to have rescuers lie prone on the ice, forming a human chain to the victim.

As soon as the victim is out of the water, he must be warmed and dried as soon as possible. Replace mittens and cap with dry ones. Get him out of the wind. Then (and not before) remove shoes and socks. Put on dry socks and replace boots, but tie loosely. Help him remove all the clothing layers under his parka and replace them if spares are at hand. Replace the parka. Keep the victim active, because an inactive person will start to chill quickly. Improvise a shelter or put up a tent. Get a stove going inside the tent to keep the victim warm. Make use of body heat from others in the party.

Replacement of clothes other than mittens or cap must be done with the assistance of another person. The victim will be too chilled; clothing may soon start to freeze. Note, however, that frozen outer clothing, such as the parka, gives good protection against wind. Fully soaked clothes may take one or two days to dry on the body.

AVALANCHE HAZARDS

An avalanche is a mass of snow moving down a mountainside, sometimes mixed with broken and uprooted trees, boulders and brush. It may be as slow as molasses—or it may be moving more than 100 mph. It can maim, crush, suffocate and kill. Only a few of those caught in a sizable avalanche have survived.

Avalanches do occur in the Eastern mountain areas,[20] including short, steep slopes that are not among high peaks. Generally they occur in remote places and do no harm, but when man and avalanche do meet, the threat to life and property is serious. In the East, with the growing influx of winter hikers into remote areas, the threat is increasing. At least two deaths have been caused by avalanches in New York State and three in the White Mountains. In another instance, hikers caught in an avalanche in the Green Mountains escaped without fatalities.

Winter mountaineers should be able to recognize avalanche terrain and should be aware of the snow conditions that may produce avalanches. Some knowledge of the mechanics of snow—crystals and bonding, transformation and accumulation during the season, wind and temperature effects, and effects of terrain on its motion—will help. Yet one never really knows when an avalanche will take place. Conditions keep changing. Thus climbers in Tuckerman and Huntington ravines on Mt. Washington and in areas immediately adjacent to it must be guided by official avalanche forecasts. On the basis of these forecasts these areas may be closed to skiers and hikers. If the areas are open, the U.S. Forest Service Snow Ranger and ski patrolman on duty there are available for advice and assistance.

Development of an avalanche depends principally upon:

1. Angle of the slope, its cover and the nature of the surface of the underlying snow or ground.
2. Depth of the snow; and
3. Character of the snow, which in turn depends on weather, temperature, exposure and wind.

On steep mountain slopes snow tends to be cleared off by gravity and wind before it gets deep. On slopes of lesser pitch it tends to accumulate, layer upon layer. As depth increases, the topmost layers have a growing tendency to move downslope. For a time the cohesive bond between layers usually holds the mass, depending on factors such as age of the snow, smoothness of the underlying stable snow and temperature of surfaces between layers. Resistance to movement can be overcome by the weight of a new snowfall or by a decrease in the holding resistance at the top, sides and bottom of the snow mass.

Resistance near the top of a slope is critical. Stretching occurs there, and the top is usually the first part to give way. This puts an increased load on the bottom, sides and intersurfaces. A slide may result—or, instead, the snow mass may merely shift downward to a point of greater resistance or stability.

Generally, avalanching occurs on slopes of 25 to 60 degrees. It can occur on grades outside this range, but the probability decreases as level ground or a vertical pitch is approached. Actual field tests suggest that the slope of greatest danger is 30 to 33 degrees.

A slab on a convex slope has a greater tendency to avalanche than one on a concave slope. Convexity adds to the tension caused by creeping. Shape of the slope is not, however, an important factor in avalanches of loose snow.

Other factors being equal, avalanches are more likely on smooth slopes than on rough ones. On the rough, rocky terrain of New York-New England mountains a considerable filling of depressions is necessary before the ground can become relatively smooth. Until then, avalanche risk is minimal. Where, however, the ground under the snow is relatively smooth—as is

Fig. 74 — Slab and loose-snow avalanches.

often the case above treeline—the probabilities of an avalanche are greater, increasing with snow depth and the other factors mentioned.

Lee slopes can be more hazardous because of the tendency of snow to pile up there in drifts. Wind action on the windward slope compacts snow and usually does not permit thick layering; hence layers there are likely to be more stable.

Snow on south-facing slopes is most exposed to the sun and hence changes more rapidly into old snow than does snow on northern slopes. As spring approaches, a southern slope may have wet-snow avalanches on account of melting between layers.

Another serious hazard is the development of a snow slab. Whereas a wet, loose snow avalanche starts in a small area, a slab avalanche begins as a large area. Slab avalanches cannot be identified with any particular type of snow crystals or snow condition. They develop with new snow as well as old, dry snow and wet snow. Slab formation is hastened by drifting and by wind action in general. It is important to remember that slab conditions can develop if changes within snow layers cause the topmost layers to come under considerable downward stress. Slab avalanches may be predicted sometimes by digging a hole and noting the condition of the layer or crust (slab layer) marking the boundary between the slab on top and its supporting snow.

Avalanches can be triggered by hikers and climbers, new snowfalls, falling snow cornices or rocks, or small snowslides. They can result from gradual action of winds, temperature and changes in the snow blanket.

Important points about the avalanche hazard can be summarized briefly:

1. No one can tell when a slide will occur.
2. We usually cannot accurately predict mountain weather—for example, make an estimate of precipitation within the next 8 hours.
3. The mountaineer should not venture into any area where slides are possible, unless with experienced leaders. Don't cross an avalanche slope; cross below or above it—preferably above it.
4. If caught in an avalanche, get rid of pack, ski poles, snowshoes and other gear immediately and start a vigorous swimming motion. Try to get out of the main slide path. Keep the feet at the surface if possible. To avoid suffocation, cover mouth and nose. Since wet avalanched snow usually freezes on settling, one's head should be kept above the surface if possible. When the slide stops, try to make an air space around head and chest.

If you are a lucky survivor and one or more of your friends in the party are buried, mark the spot where the victims were last seen. Make a hasty search of the area below this point for bits of equipment, clothing, etc. — signs that would indicate their positions. Investigate and mark any clues. Do not rush off for help without taking these steps. To do so could mean loss of life that otherwise could have been saved by a rescue party.

YOUR CAR IN COLD WEATHER

Cold weather, even the relatively mild cold weather of Boston or New York, can make an engine stubborn. It gets even more stubborn in mountain country where the temperature minimums are substantially lower.

Before a winter trip a car must be prepared:

1. Tune up the engine, and check especially the choke operation, belts, and hoses.
2. Check battery (clean posts with coarse steel wool and scrape inside cable connectors with a pocket knife), voltage regulator and generator or alternator. Replace a worn-out battery. An extra-heavy-duty battery installed in your car will help materially. See that the battery is fully charged.
3. Use low temperature engine oil—the lowest for the temperature anticipated. SAE 10 oil makes much easier starting than SAE 20 when the temperature is 20 below. Check with your car dealer or garage on the proper oil.
4. Add 3 cans of "dry gas" to your gas tank to prevent frozen fuel lines, or put in premium gas if you ordinarily use regular gas.

The AAA Road Service has stated that some cars do not start in cold weather because the cold causes the butterfly valve, which is connected to the choke and aids in regulating the air-fuel mix, to stick. Another source stated that pressing the accelerator pedal all the way to the floor is likely to loosen a frozen choke. After taking this action, follow normal starting procedure. A shot of ether in the carburetor air intake may help.

When preparing your car for the winter or for a trip to low temperature mountain areas, consider a synthetic lubricating oil such as "Mobil 1." The cost can be as much as five times that of best quality mineral oil, but because of greater low temperature viscosity, the engine starting problem is substantially reduced. Other advantages, like improved operation at high engine temperature, are cited by manufacturers. Synthetic oils made to government specifications are used in arctic military equipment.

The cranking power of a battery is greatly affected by temperature. If the battery was not fully charged, don't be surprised if it will not turn the crankshaft at 20 below. Table 13 shows the effect of temperature and state of charge on cranking power.

Keep battery cables in your car so that you can boost the battery power if necessary. Connect the cables to the battery of another car in parallel (positive to positive, negative to negative). If you suspect corrosion between posts and cable connectors, press the booster cables by hand directly to the tops of the posts.

TABLE 13
Effect of Temperature and State of Charge on Cranking Power of Battery[5]

Temperature		Cranking Power of Lead-acid Battery		
°F	°C	Fully Charged	Half-Charged	Nearly Discharged
80	26.9	100%	46%	25%
32	0	65	32	16
0	17.9	40	21	9

Fig. 75 shows some of the winter accessories (in addition to a shovel and a bucket of sand) you should think about carrying:

a. *A set of strap-on chains (at least two) with wire threader.* You cannot rely entirely on snow tires for traction in mud or snow. If your rear hubs have slots or holes in the rims, these chains are most useful. The wire is passed through the hubs from the inside so that the chains can be secured on the outside.

b. *Skid chains.* When the snow is exceptionally deep, or traction is otherwise difficult, these chains can keep you going. To attach them it is necessary to jack the wheels off the ground or use a slotted ramp.

c. *Tow chain with a hook at each end.* If you are stuck, and if another car or truck with traction is available, pass the chain or cable around a solid part underneath each vehicle in a short loop, then attach the hook to a chain link or around the cable. Do not secure the hook directly.

d. *Ice scraper.* Necessary for removing ice and hard snow from your windows.

e. *Brush.* Useful for getting snow off the car.

Other advice to consider:

Be sure sand is dry when loaded into your car, or it may freeze solid. Instead of sand you can use cat litter.

You may have the problem of unlocking your frozen door, trunk or panel locks. A squirt of ethyl or isopropyl alcohol into the lock may solve the problem. To deter freezing, spray a light oil such as WD-40 into your locks. Avoid locking the car in the first place if possible.

Tests by the Canada Safety Council have demonstrated that as the temperature approaches zero, the friction provided by snow tires or chains on icy roads becomes less significant — in other words, nearly worthless. Final reminder: be sure you

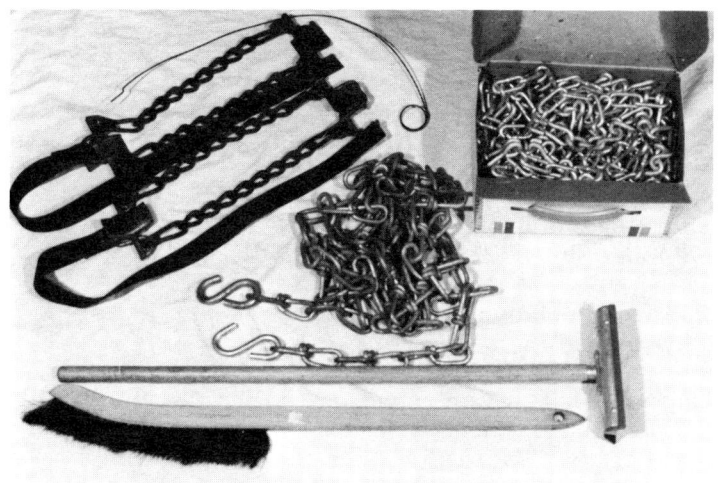

Fig. 75 —Snow country accessories: Strap-on chains with wire, skid chains, tow chain, scraper, brush.

have a working defroster, windshield defrosting fluid and sufficient anti-freeze protection.

Good luck!

HIKING AND SKI TOURING AREAS

One need not drive hundreds of miles to go skiing or snowshoeing. A local park may be suitable. But, particularly if you are a city dweller, the most complete enjoyment comes from taking a trip to the mountains to ski on old tote roads, fire roads, lakes, rivers and streambeds, and hiking and ski trails, including the commercial ski touring centers with graded trails that have proliferated in recent years. The Catskills, Adirondacks, Green Mountains, White Mountains, and Katahdin area of Maine are the most significant winter sports sections of New York and New England.

Parties often consist of both skiers and snowshoers. One can be both a "shoer" and a skier by carrying skis while climbing upgrade on snowshoes in anticipation of returning down on the skis.

148 TRAVEL

Although it is possible to organize your own winter party, for continuous enjoyment over the years it is better and simpler to join a hiking club and participate in its winter activities. If you are not a club member and want information about a club or chapter of a club, consider contacting these organizations in your area:

Adirondack Mountain Club
172 Ridge Street, Glens Falls, N.Y. 12801

Appalachian Mountain Club
5 Joy Street, Boston, Mass. 02108

Finger Lakes Trail Conference
P.O. Box 18048
Rochester, N.Y. 14618

Green Mountain Club
108 Merchants Row, Rutland, Vt. 05701

New York/New Jersey Trail Conference
20 West 40th Street, New York, N.Y. 10018

For interesting trails and areas for winter hiking and ski touring, consult the guide books listed in the Appendix. Some of these sources, such as the Ski Touring Guide published by the Ski Touring Council, contain specific information — descriptions of routes, sketch maps, degree of difficulty, precautions, etc.

Shelter

ASSUME A PARTY expects to ascend a mountain and camp there overnight in two-man tents. Poles are carried so that the tents can be set up anywhere. Travel to the site is timed so that the party arrives in daylight. There is time to put up the tents, prepare meals and get set for the night.

PLACING AND SECURING THE TENT

There are no hard-and-fast rules for placing tents. You may wish to pitch your tent for a good view of the surrounding country. If high wind is a possibility, set the tent up in the woods or among large boulders if available. If you camp in a windy, exposed place, the constant flapping of the tent fabric can keep the occupants awake all night; if you camp under a tree, heavy snow accumulations may fall on your tent. Some snow can be knocked off the trees with ski poles, skis, or ice ax.

Firm the snow on the site by stamping with your feet, snowshoes, or skis. For a more comfortable night's sleep, excavate a cavity in the snow for your hips before erecting the tent. Place the tent broadside to the wind so that the entrance can be kept clear of snow. In open areas, don't camp in a lee. If you do, drifting snow may bury you.

If in an exposed position, use a snow-block wall or excavate a site for your tent. The problem with the latter is that snow may drift into the site and completely cover your tent, and the tent may collapse unless the snow is removed every 3 to 4 hours. But it may be better to do this than be exposed to severe wind.

Tent stakes may be useless unless they can be driven into hard snow or frozen ground. Use stakes that will stand the pounding. Your ice ax, skis, or ski poles can be useful here too. For a tent anchor you can use a "dead man," consisting of a branch placed horizontally deep in the snow. Tie your guy line to it, then stamp the snow firmly over it. If your tent has a snow flap, place rocks or snow or ice blocks on it. If possible do not tie the guy line to the "dead man." Instead loop the line around it so that when the tent is taken down the line can be pulled out.

Are your tent poles sectional? To avoid losing a section in the snow, connect each with shock cord or elastic.

SHELTER 151

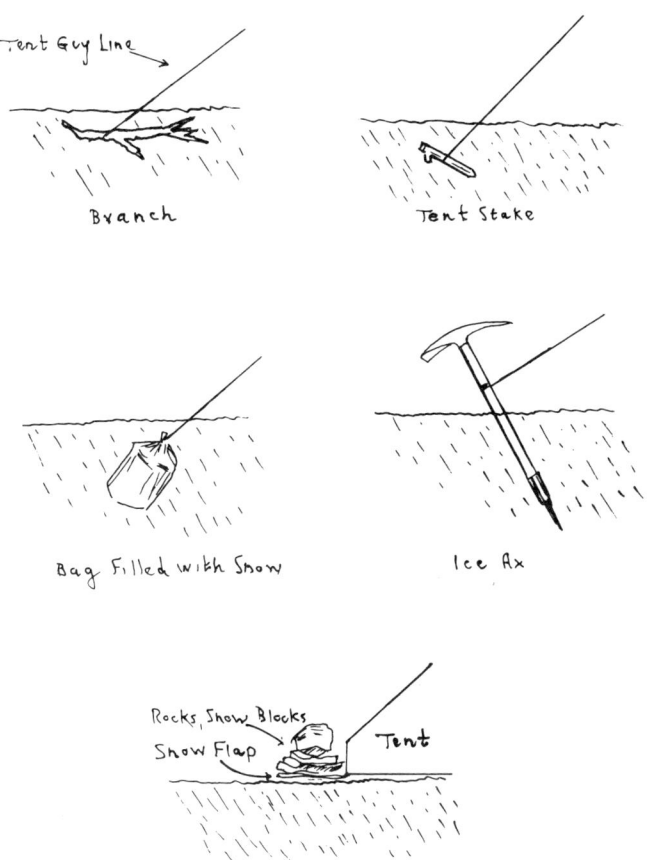

Fig. 76 — Methods of securing a tent.

Inside the tent stretch out your sleeping bag on top of a thick foam pad or air mattress plus at least a ½ in. foam pad. Stow your packs inside. Some tents do not have enough room for a pack, in which case they have to be left outside. Tie a tent guy or a separate line to the packs so that they will not blow away and can be located in a drift. Before entering the tent, brush all snow off your clothing.

GETTING DINNER

The next question is whether to cook or not to cook. If possible, eat a hot meal. If the weather does not permit cooking, eat cold food — perhaps a duplication of your lunch — while in your sleeping bag. Wash it down with a hot drink. If cooking is practicable, set up your stove on a heat-resistant board in the vestibule or inside the tent in the cookhole. If inside, be sure to have sufficient ventilation to disperse water vapor and to prevent carbon-monoxide accumulation. If the weather permits cooking outside, protect your stove from the wind.

Use a pot to melt snow or ice. If snow is powdery, melt a little first, then gradually add more. This method will avoid a burned pot bottom. Burning will not occur if the snow or ice is wet. Wet snow for water is better than powder snow or ice, because it melts faster, makes more water and needs less heat.

Make enough water for your evening meal and breakfast. Put the breakfast water in your vacuum bottle or canteen. A canteen can be kept from freezing by keeping it inside your sleeping bag or in an insulated hole dug under your sleeping bag—if this can be done in your tent. Another method is to bury a pot of water, with lid, in a hole just outside the tent entrance. Cover the pot with about 12 in. of loose snow. The water will be ready for use in the morning even if the temperature goes down to −30°F. One hiker melts snow in the evening for his breakfast water, then stows the pot inside a partly filled bag of snow. The water remains liquid for breakfast.

After getting water, start the one-pot glop planned for that evening, plus hot soup, beverages and other delights. The meal should be pioneering simplicity itself.

No fussing! You checked out your stove before the trip. You know exactly where to find your food in the pack.

A simple system for packing food is to put each meal in a plastic bag marked in big letters — DINNER, NIBBLE, BREAKFAST. Dehydrated main-course foods take longer to prepare and require a good part of your small water supply, but they are light. They should be tested at home before the trip, so that you will know how to prepare them properly.

Fuel can be conserved by cooking the meal in one pot with a slightly larger pot placed over it for a lid. Snow can be put in the upper pot for melting. Covering the food will prevent it from producing large clouds of vapor.

Don't be fastidious about washing cup and pot. Learn to tolerate a little soup, dessert, and glop mixed with hot chocolate.

BEDDING DOWN

Enough has been said about sleeping bags and the need for insulation underneath. Most hikers today use either a closed cell or open cell foam pad. An air mattress does not provide sufficient insulation by itself; its air space is too large. The more you move, the more the air circulates. Place a foam pad or extra clothing between bag and mattress.

Don't curl up in the bottom of your bag. Leave your face out so that vapor from your breath does not get into the down.

Don't worry about freezing while asleep. Your body is a dependable thermostat. If body temperature goes down too much, you will wake up.

BREAKING CAMP

Collapse your tent and roll it while it is still warm, or the tent floor will freeze to the ground. If it does freeze, strips of waterproofing will be ripped off while you are rolling it up.

MAKING A SNOWHOUSE

To acquire experience in primitive polar living, a party can plan to construct a snowhouse or two or more interconnecting snowhouses. This can be done in an area where the snow is packed to the right consistency. In the New York-New England area, however, a snowhouse should not be considered a practical emergency measure. It takes at least two hours for two skilled campers to construct one, and a lot of energy is burned up. In any case, the snow usually cannot be cut into blocks.

Fig. 77 shows in cross-section the basic features of a snowhouse. Note the protected underground entrance, the sleeping shelf above the floor, and the vent. Each block is about 36 in. long, 18 in. wide, and 6 in. thick, and shaped so that it inclines inward and the lower perpendicular edge butts firmly against the preceding block.

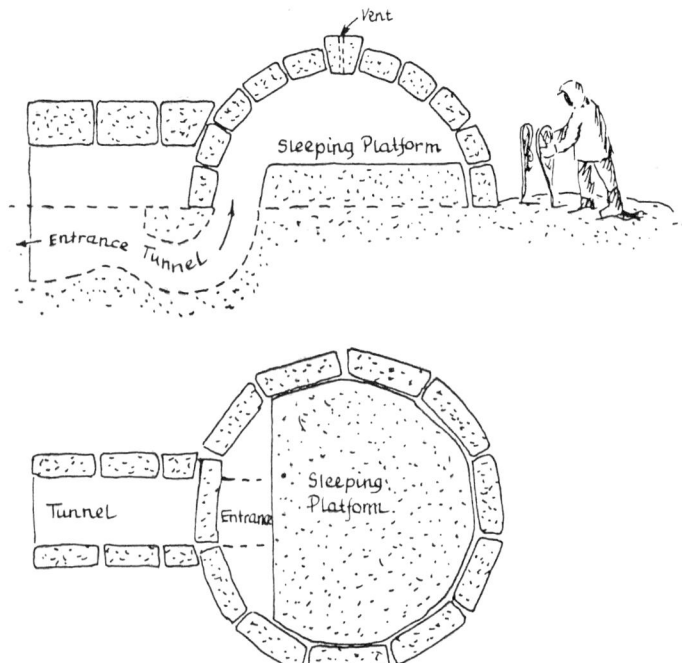

Fig. 77 —Design of a snowhouse.

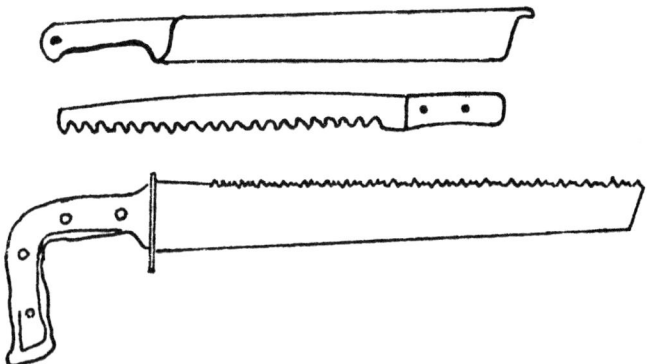

Fig. 78 —Types of snow knives.

SHELTER 155

To build a snowhouse use a snow knife, saw, or machete. Fig. 79 shows the phases and methods of construction. Note the temporary access hole which must be cut so that one man can place blocks from the inside in the later stages. The last step is to fit the key block in top center. After the entrance is made, a stove can be ignited for a short period to melt the interior surface. Upon freezing the snowhouse will be appreciably stronger — capable of supporting the weight of several men. After the chinks are filled on the outside, additional snow can be piled on for better insulation. Care must be taken to avoid overheating the interior.

Fig. 79 —Stages in construction of a snowhouse.[36]

156   SHELTER

A partially completed snowhouse (Adirondacks)

MAKING A SNOW-MOUND HOUSE

When the party is not experienced in building a snow (block) house, or snow cannot be cut into blocks, it is possible to build a shelter from loose snow. Fig. 80 shows a four-man shelter. Subarctic Indians of North America, such as the Athapaskans and Chipewyans, construct snow-mound shelters, "Quinzhees," on account of the loose, fluffy snow common to the region.[54]

In the selected spot, place an upright marker (stick, ski pole, ice ax, rock) to mark the center. Tie a cord to the marker and scribe a circle in the snow to indicate the pile size. Rule of thumb for size: if snow in place is not to be dug out, radius should be the interior size plus about 2 ft. (61 cm.); if snow in place is to be dug out, about 1 ft. (30 cm.) can be subtracted from the radius for each foot of in-place snow. Piling the mound will take two men about an hour for a two-man shelter.

Now pile loose snow within the circle with shovels, tarp, and anything else handy. Don't compact the snow. When the mound is of the right size and shape, do not disturb it; allow it to compact naturally — minimum time one hour. Chances of collapse are greatly reduced after letting it settle for two hours. After compaction you are ready to start digging.

SHELTER 157

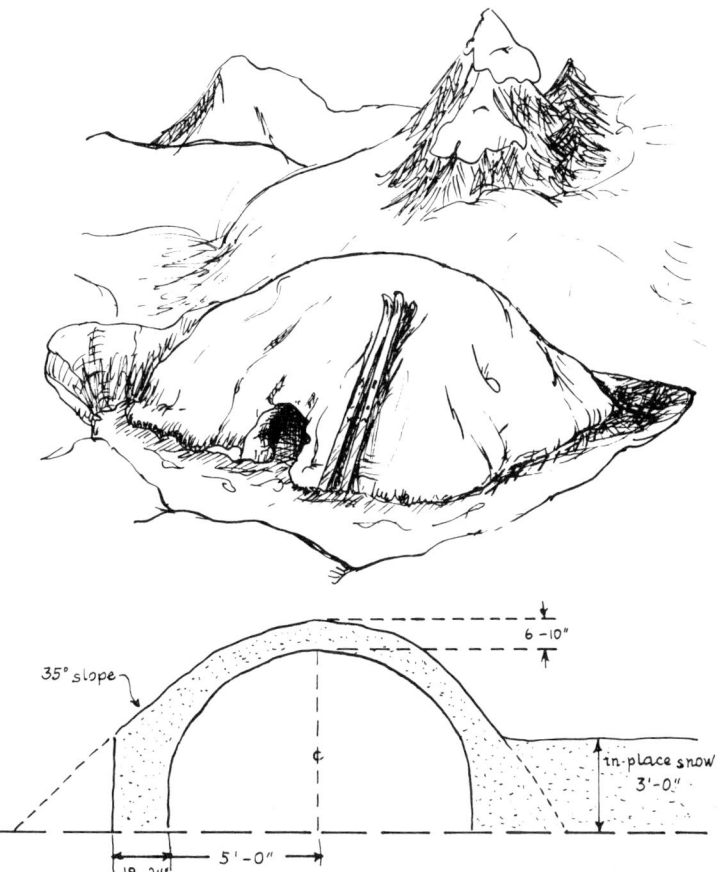

Fig. 80—Snow-mound house and design for four persons.

From the entrance point start digging toward the marker. Pass the snow to your partner on the outside. As soon as the marker is reached, do not disturb it; this is your guide for excavating the interior. Swing your ice ax or ski pole in arcs around the marker, not greater than the intended radius. To check on the wall and roof thickness, measure with a stick or wire pushed through them. When the dimensions check, remove the marker and trim the interior. Then install a vent in the roof. Get rid of waste snow outside promptly—before it hardens.

158   SHELTER

Thirty-five degrees is the natural angle at which loose snow rests. Be sure to allow the snow to settle at this angle. If you don't, you will have problems — thin spots or windows, or a buckling roof when you dig out the interior.

The mining involved will tend to wet your clothing—another problem.

Snow-mound houses: (Top) National Cold Weather Camping Development Center, Boy Scouts of America (Minnesota)

(Bottom) Adirondacks

Finding Position and Directions

MAP AND COMPASS

A WINTER HIKER should have a compass for efficient cross-country navigation and personal safety. One must know how to use a compass; practice using it. If familiar with the area, you may not need to use a map, but a compass is needed to maintain a course. To go the wrong way could have serious consequences.

The leader or some other person in a party should have a U.S. Geological Survey topographical map, usually 1:62,500 (about 1 in. to the mile) with trails overprinted. Most topo maps show only well-established trails. Before the trip, mark the other trails also on the topo map, using the information from your guide book. The Adirondack Mountain Club marks trails on topo sheets for certain areas of New York State. Maps included in the Appalachian Mountain Club's "White Mountain Guide" are excellent. In well-traveled areas you can get along safely with a guide book only, but it is best to use a topo map showing trails.

Map reading, like reading white water from a canoe, requires close attention to detail. Roads, streams, and other small features must be related from the map to the ground, and vice versa. Be able to mentally convert the two-dimensional map into three-dimensional relief — mountains, valleys, cliffs, ridges, cols, steep and gradual slopes. Learn to distinguish landforms, vegetation, and works of man—particularly roads.

Study your map at home—at leisure and in detail. Learn the trail system and the trail markers. Most of the time you will be using trails, but deep snow, and accumulated ice, snow, or rime on trees may here and there have obliterated the route.

Learn to visualize the terrain from contour lines. For practice, try drawing a mountain and a valley cross-section to scale from a map. Draw a line through a segment and drop perpendiculars to a series of horizontal lines for each contour interval (usually 20 ft. on New York-New England maps).

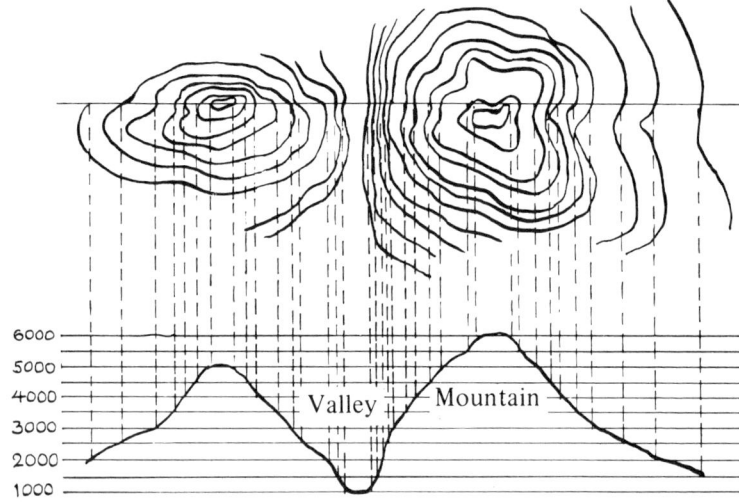

Fig. 81 —Visualizing a terrain from contour lines.

CROSS-COUNTRY NAVIGATION

To follow a cross-country course, first determine the magnetic direction from your position to your destination. Then sight in this direction to a distant tree, rock, or other distinctive object. Repeat this process from object to object until the destination is reached. On the way, detours around gullies, cliffs, swamps, or other obstructions may be required.

If your destination is on or near a natural baseline such as a stream, river, lake, or ridge, it is often better to get a bearing on a point to the right or left of the destination. When you reach the baseline, you will then definitely know the direction to go. For example, if on the return leg of your hike you took a bearing on your camp near an unfamiliar road, you might be confused about the direction to go on reaching the road.

To get a magnetic bearing (azimuth), orient the map so that it corresponds with the ground. Place the compass on or adjacent to the declination diagram at the bottom of the map. Twist the map until magnetic north on it corresponds with the compass needle; the map is now oriented. If the map does not show

FINDING POSITION AND DIRECTIONS   161

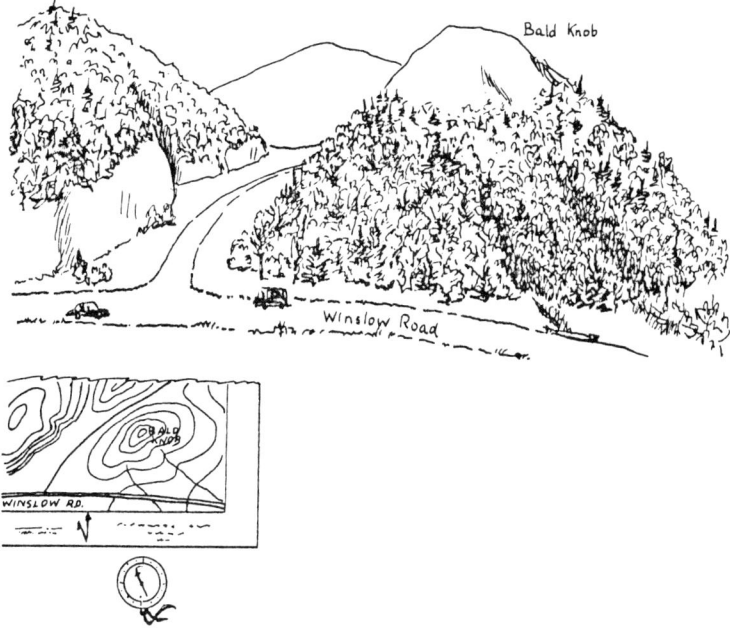

Fig. 82 —Orienting a map with a compass: Map is placed so needle of compass (below) is parallel to magnetic deviation line on map.

magnetic north in a declination diagram or otherwise, then twist the map right or left for declination. (In New York-New England area magnetic north is west of true north, so move the map clockwise for the amount of declination.) Without the compass a map can also be oriented less accurately by aligning with identifiable mountains, rivers, lakes, or other features.

Once the map is oriented, magnetic bearings can be taken between any points on it. These bearings can be converted, if desired, to true north bearings by correcting for the declination angle. (In New York-New England, subtract.) For local travel one should not convert each magnetic bearing to true north bearing, because a precise calculation does not necessarily make your course more accurate. Forget about declination, except to orient the map as explained, unless you are plotting an extensive course through an area where the declination change may otherwise introduce an appreciable error. A change of one degree would put you about 1/5 mi. off in a 10-mi. course; in 50 mi. the compass error would be about one mile!

For local travel, then, obtain a magnetic bearing and take off. Be sure you know your location on the map. Trace your course on the map by following dead-reckoning procedure; that is, estimate your distance and direction on each straight-line leg. When you change direction, note your position on the map. Check your course by taking a back bearing on your last point. Associate your course with a natural baseline such as a ridge, river, stream, or two or more peaks.

A party can maintain a direction reasonably well, without continuous reference to landmarks, by marching in single file. The separation between members should be as great as visibility permits. The rear man is the navigator and orders the column to bear right or left to maintain direction. This method is useful above treeline or where visibility is poor.

DETERMINING POSITION

Ordinarily, determining position simply involves checking progress along an established trail. If the trail you are on cannot be identified, your location can be determined by reference to surrounding peaks, valleys, rivers, lakes, and other objects against your oriented map. If in doubt, check topographic features on reaching a high point; climb to an overlook if necessary for a good view.

Accurate self-location can be done by taking magnetic bearings on two prominent features at least 90 degrees apart. On your map draw back-bearing lines from these points. The intersection of the lines is your position. As a check, take a bearing on a third feature.

A quick, easy way to get your approximate position is to sight along a straight stick placed on your oriented map through a mountain and toward the corresponding distant peak. Draw a line on the map along the sighted stick. Repeat the process for the second mountain. The intersection of the two lines is your approximate position. (See Fig. 83.)

If your party has a calibrated altimeter, your position and progress along a slope can be approximately determined.

FINDING POSITION AND DIRECTIONS 163

Fig. 83—Straight-stick method of determining position.

While moving along a trail, note your elevation in relation to the intersection of the contour lines and the trail.

When on a peak, use map and compass to identify surrounding peaks, valleys, streams, or other features. This practice will improve your knowledge of the area.

Such knowledge can be helpful. Many mountain systems have a fairly consistent linear structure, shown by the direction of most of the ridges. Before embarking on a trip, study a topographical or relief map and note the basic features—particularly the drainage patterns.

If the direction of the prevailing wind among the peaks is known, you may be able to tell directions from the rime on trees. Trees in exposed locations on peaks generally have a thicker rime accumulation on the windward side. Note these indicators in exposed areas as you ascend. They will help you get back to the trail, particularly when weather conditions do not permit compass sightings.

DIRECTIONS FROM SUN, STARS, AND MOON

Primitive peoples such as the Indians, Polynesians, and others who lived close to the land did not have compasses, but they knew their directions. They could find their way during the

164 FINDING POSITION AND DIRECTIONS

Cairns not totally buried by snow guide a hiker across the Alpine Garden on Mt. Washington.

White out... Which way to go?

hunt, knew the direction of unseen land, traveled in fog, made tremendous voyages across the Pacific. The winter hiker or climber, no less than these peoples, may have to use his wits and know-how to get back to a lodge, camp, or other starting point safely. If other direction-finding methods are not available, he may be able to rely upon the sun, stars, and moon.

The Sun as a Guide

In winter in the north temperate zone the sun will rise south of east and sets south of west. But at noon by your watch, the sun is due south (if your location is the middle of your time zone).

The angles the sun makes at 45 degrees north latitude from rising to setting are indicated in Table 14. For example, at 10 a.m. on January 16 the sun will be 150 degrees from true north, or 60 degrees south of east. On the same date the rising sun has a bearing of 120 degrees.

TABLE 14
Angles of the Sun at 45° North Latitude[28]

Hours from noon	Sep. 23 Mar. 21	Oct. 4 Mar. 11	Oct. 14 Mar. 1	Oct. 25 Feb. 18	Nov. 3 Feb. 9	Nov. 14 Jan. 29	Nov. 27 Jan. 16	Dec. 11 Jan. 2
0	180	180	180	180	180	180	180	180
1	159	161	162	163	163	164	165	165
2	141	143	145	147	148	149	150	151
3	125	128	130	133	134	136	137	139
4	112	115	118	120	122	124	126	127
5	101	104	106	109	—	—	—	—
6	90	—	—	—	—	—	—	—
Rise & Set	90	96	101	107	111	116	120	124

Directions by the Stars

Acquaint yourself with the constellations of the winter sky so that you can tell immediately the general direction you are facing. The sky chart may be helpful to learn or relearn the most conspicuous constellations, particularly those of the southern winter sky. On looking at the actual sky the winter hiker and skier quickly notices its clarity; this is due to the drier air. The southern winter sky is particularly prominent on account of the number of the most brilliant stars:

Rigel and Betelgeuse in Orion
Sirius (the brightest) in Big Dog
Capella in Charioteer (Auriga)
Pollux in Twins (Gemini)
Procyon in Little Dog
Aldebaron in Bull

166   FINDING POSITION AND DIRECTIONS

The chart is properly oriented when it is over your head. Your position is directly below the intersection of the north-south/east-west lines. The chart is also valid for January 16, 11 p.m.; February 1, 10 p.m.; February 15, 9 p.m.; March 1, 8 p.m.; and March 16, 7 p.m. For more assistance one can consult a dial star finder and home planetarium, such as Hammond's, for the daily and seasonal changes.

Constellations to notice when facing—

North: Great Bear (Ursa Major), Little Bear (Ursa Minor), Cassiopeia, Cepheus, Dragon (Draco) — all visible the entire year. *South:* Orion, Hare (Lepus), Big Dog (Canus Major), Bull (Taurus), Ram (Aries), Pleiades.

In our scouting days we learned how to locate precisely the north star (Polaris) from the pointer stars (Dubhe and Merak) in the Big Dipper. When you face Polaris, east is on your right,

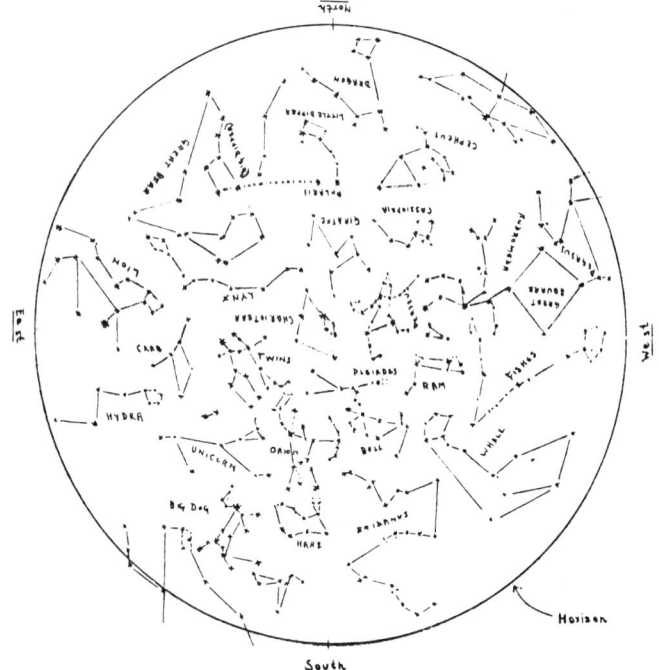

Fig. 84—Sky chart on January 1, 12 midnight, 40° north.

FINDING POSITION AND DIRECTIONS 167

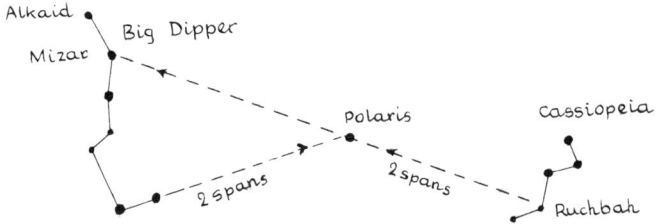

Fig. 85 —Directions from Cassiopeia and Big Dipper: Star patterns are unchanged as they circle daily around pole star.

west on your left. The pole star, when visible, is the first fairly bright star in line with the Pointers in the direction away from the top of the Big Dipper's bowl.

Suppose you can see the Big Dipper, but the pole star is obscured. To find north, extend your arm and spread your fingers. At that moment the apparent sky distance between the middle finger and thumb is a span. The pole star is two spans from a point midway between the Pointers, or about five times the distance between these stars.

Even if the pole star is invisible, the direction of north can be determined by drawing an imaginary line between certain other stars that are not obscured. A line from the star Procyon (in Canus Minor) drawn to pass between Castor and Pollux (in Gemini) points approximately north. So does a line from Saiph through Betelgeuse (both in Orion), or from Rigel (in Orion) through Capella (in Auriga). These relationships hold at all times.

Even without reference to indicator stars, one can distinguish between east and west horizons on any clear night. Simply note whether the stars near the horizon are rising or setting. Stars rise in the east and set in the west, except for stars so near the pole star that they do not dip below the horizon at all.

These explanations about getting a direction from the north star, seen or unseen, are given for comprehensiveness. Under the usual circumstances it is unlikely that it would be necessary, or even possible, to take a bearing from the north star or an estimate of its position. In mountainous country, the hiker frequently cannot move on a precise course; he must stay on the trail. It is most important, however, that he know the

168   FINDING POSITION AND DIRECTIONS

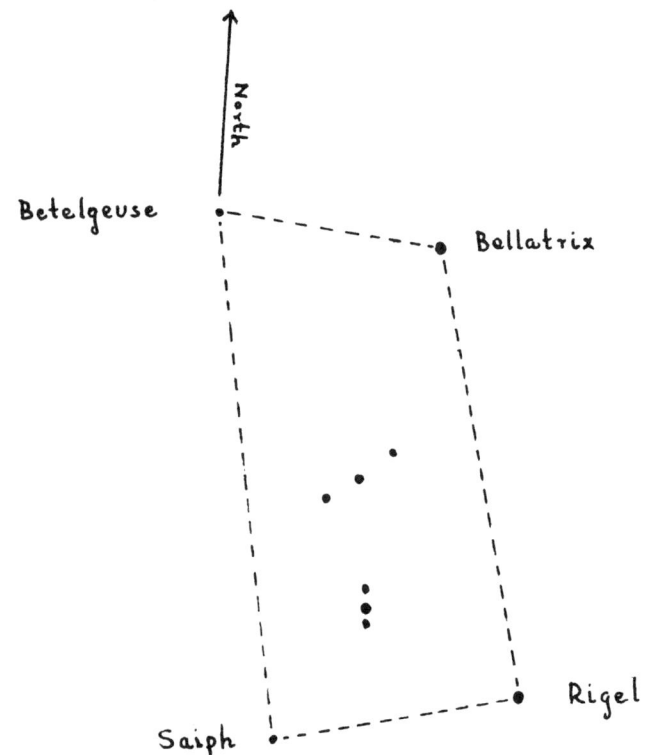

Fig. 86 —Directions from constellation Orion: Direction of north is always the same with respect to the star pattern.

general direction he should go (to the shelter, to the starting point, etc.) and get his guidance from the constellations of the northern and southern skies.

Orientation by the Moon

The moon too can indicate direction. Like the sun, the moon rises in the east, sets in the west, and is due south (for an observer in the northern hemisphere) when highest in the sky. The full moon is always opposite (180 degrees away from) the sun. When the moon is a crescent, the convex side is toward the sun.

Survival and Rescue

ANY PERSON who engages in winter mountaineering as a sport or as part of his work must be trained in techniques of survival. He must be prepared to overcome extremely trying conditions that could lead to severe frostbite if not loss of life from hypothermia. He may at any time face the task of preserving life under conditions of inadequate food, water, or shelter.

In a predicament the most important thing is to overcome fear. Fear can be so overwhelming that a situation can soon become desperate, even if adequate food, water, and shelter are at hand.

The basic rules:

1. Keep calm. Keep your wits.
2. Study the situation. Make the best judgment you can.
3. Get into an emergency shelter.

Above all, one needs the will to survive. Ultimately, whether or not one survives grave danger depends largely on one's spirit, faith, optimism, determination, guts, just plain stubbornness—or a generous mixture of all these traits.

EMERGENCY SHELTER

Suppose that because of oncoming darkness or foul weather you must spend the night out. Seek shelter well before it gets too dark to maneuver. If a lean-to or other regular shelter is nearby, get there if you can. If no such haven is available, look for a place protected from the wind—a cave, a rock overhang, a roomy crevice, a natural rock terrace.

Day hikers ordinarily don't carry a tarp. If you have one, fashion it into a tent, using branches if available. Set this up in a sheltered spot if one can be found. If in a lean-to, use the tarp to keep out wind and blowing snow.

The best shelter is one that will hold the heat of a small fire, or one in which body heat will be conserved. The shelter should be small and windproof and should have adequate ventilation to prevent asphyxiation—especially if you use a stove or build a fire.

170 FINDING POSITION AND DIRECTIONS

Fig. 87 — A snow cave under tree branches.

If time and circumstances permit, a snow cave can be built to accommodate at least two men. In wooded areas in deep snow, a cave can be dug underneath tree branches (Fig. 87).

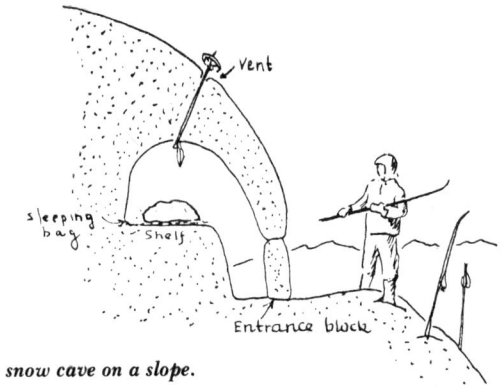

Fig. 88 — A snow cave on a slope.

A cave can be dug in a deep drift or snowbank, or into a steep slope (Fig. 88), provided you have a digging tool and the snow is not too hard. Be sure to make a vent if a stove is to be used in the cave.

FINDING POSITION AND DIRECTIONS 171

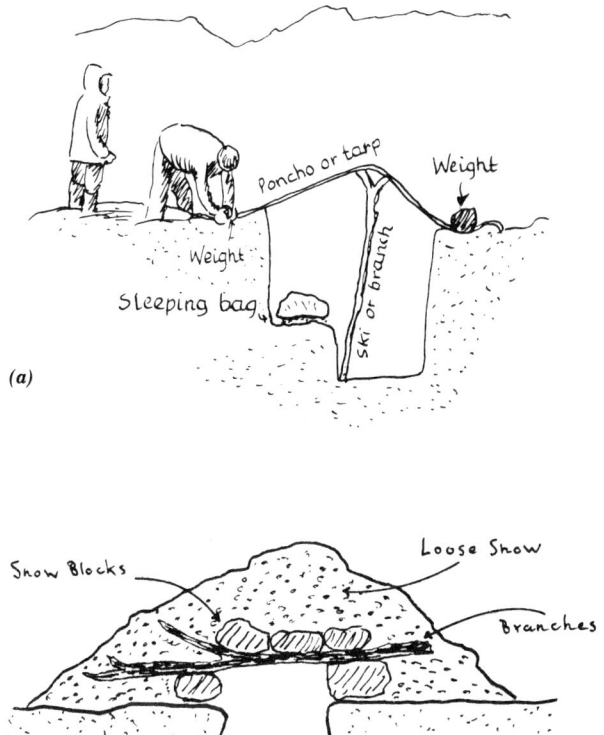

Fig. 89 — Trench shelters: (a) Covered with a poncho or tarp (b) Covered with branches, snow blocks, and loose snow.[45]

On level ground a trench shelter can be constructed. Dig a trench as illustrated and cover the top with whatever materials are available (Fig. 89).

172 FINDING POSITION AND DIRECTIONS

For the trench shelter below, excavate a body-width trench about 7 ft. long and 4½ ft. deep. Keep the top part as narrow as possible, but scoop out the sides around the bottom so that the trench is bell-shaped. Roof it over temporarily with snowshoes, or skis and poles, then pile loose snow on top. After about an hour, when the snow will have compacted, remove the temporary supports. The shelter is finished. A small wood fire can be built at one end for drying clothes and keeping warm.

EMERGENCY SIGNALS

An injured hiker or other person in need can signal with a noisy whistle (howling wind and forest noises permitting), a headlight, or a signaling mirror to attract other parties. Having the equipment to do this could mean the difference between disaster and safety.

To signal a nearby person on the ground, blow your whistle three times in succession, and repeat at regular intervals. The other party should acknowledge the distress signal by blowing his whistle two times quickly in succession, and likewise repeating at regular intervals. Use your headlight, signaling mirror, or contrasting items visible from the air, such as clothing or branches, in a three-series signal.

To make a signaling mirror, drill a ¼-in. hole in the center of a camper's metal mirror—the kind with a reflecting surface on both sides. When using the mirror, hold it as shown (Fig. 90) for a target which is more or less in the direction of the sun.

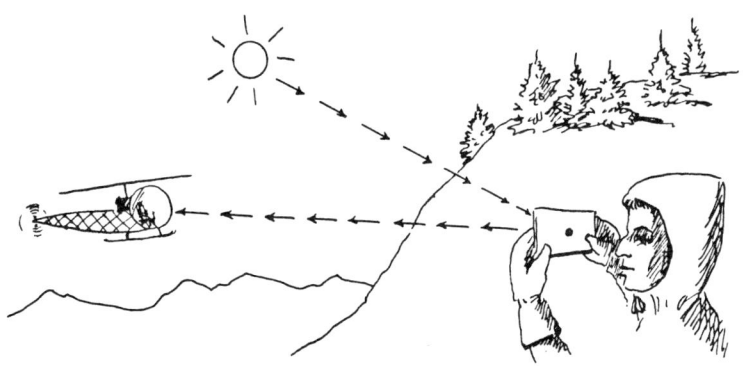

Fig. 90 — The signaling mirror.

Note the spot of sunlight on your face. Change the mirror angle so that the spot will coincide with the hole and the target (aircraft or ground party). Then the sunlight is reflected to the target. If the angle between sun, yourself, and the target is so great that you do not see any spot on your face, extend your hand. You will see the spot there. Make the same alignment as before. Wiggle the mirror to make a flashing signal. Another aiming method, using a mirror without a hole in the center, is described in *The Complete Walker* by Colin Fletcher.

174 FINDING POSITION AND DIRECTIONS

Simple messages can be sent to aircraft flying overhead. The messages are expressed in symbols. Those in Fig. 91 are standard. They should be 8 to 10 ft. long and can be fashioned by trampling the snow, arranging logs or tree branches, or making patterns with snow on an adjacent snowless area. Trampled symbols can be made more visible by filling the grooves with branches. You may want to use body signals (see Fig. 92).

Fig. 92 — Body signals to an aircraft.

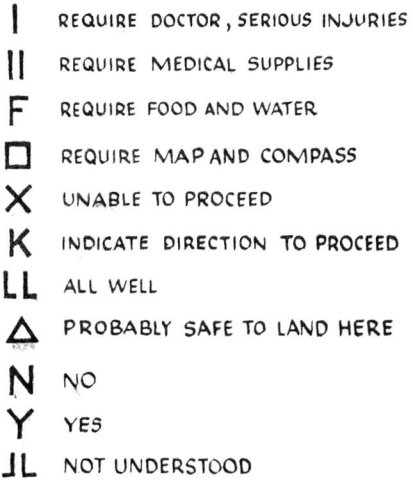

Fig. 91 —Ground-to-air signals.

EMERGENCY HEAT

In a wooded area it may be possible to build a fire. This may require much time and effort, depending on the circumstances. Without matches the prospect is practically hopeless.

It may save your life to have non-safety matches in your kit. They should be waterproofed and in a watertight container. Cement a piece of sandpaper to the container. Anything to minimize the fuss of firebuilding is important.

Build a fire on short logs as illustrated (Fig. 93) if the snow is deep; otherwise clear away the snow down to the earth. Use fire-starters (the ready-made ones or the kind made of rolled newspaper tied with string and soaked in paraffin); or use a candle. Birch bark or fuzz sticks could help. Pile on dead branches ("Indian kerosene") broken off surrounding trees. Coniferous wood will burn easier because of the resin.

For a party of not more than three, a small fire could be adequate. Not much wood is needed to keep it going, and the party can get fairly close to it. For a bigger group make an

Fig. 93 — A fire can be built on logs laid in the snow.

elongated fire so that all party members can get near it. Some heat will be reflected if a fire is built against a vertical rock face or in front of an emergency fabric lean-to. Don't waste time making a log reflector; it does not reflect, and it blocks access to one side of the fire. Avoid wasting energy cutting wood; let the fire shorten it for you. Start burning each log at the end and keep pushing the logs toward the center of the fire as they shorten.

Heat from a wood fire, stove, candle, or even body heat will be conserved if an emergency shelter is available. Note in the discussion of microclimate how a single candle can increase the temperature in a shelter if a door — a tarp or other covering — closes the entrance.

EMERGENCY FOOD

Another source of heat is food. In winter mountaineering always have extra food in your pack for emergency situations, even on short day hikes — candy bar, fruit-nut bar, extra sandwich, remainder of your hot drink, and the like. If you have means of heating the food, so much the better; heating may be necessary if your extras are frozen. Some items can be eaten even when frozen.

Reminder—
Even for a one-day hike the following "minimum" survival items should be carried:

"Strike anywhere" matches, waterproofed, in container
Candle
Pocketknife—sharpened
First-aid kit
Signaling mirror
Whistle
Flashlight
Fire-starters
Sleeping bag
Compass and map

Refer also to the checklist of individual equipment.

RESCUE

Be prepared for a time when an injured or ill person, high on a mountain, may have to be evacuated to a lodge or other heated shelter where he can be given adequate care and from which he can be taken to a hospital if necessary.

Suppose the emergency happens in your party. Give the victim first aid and follow the precautions previously mentioned for frostbite, hypothermia, and other conditions. If available, two persons capable of the effort should be dispatched to get an excavation party with carrier, such as a basket litter, toboggan or pulk (a boatlike sled) and, if necessary, medical assistance. When going for help the two should take with them:

1. Written notes as to condition of victim, location of injury, drugs or medications carried by the party (in case a doctor is found to send advice to the rescue party).
2. Map showing location of victim.

On arrival at a lodge or other source of help, give the ranger or state police all details, including notes and map, name and address of victim, number and names of other party members, party member who is caring for the victim, and the nature of the help needed.

An evacuation party should be made up of persons experienced and capable of making an emergency trip to a remote wilderness point in deep snow and extreme cold. Such persons may be found in the local volunteer mountain rescue group or among local members of a mountain club. The party could be assisted by the state police or forest rangers and further aided by plane or helicopter. The evacuation of even one injured person requires the cooperation of many people.

An effective evacuation party might include an evacuation leader, a rescue team and leader, and a support team and leader. The rescue team—guided, if possible, by one member of the hiking party who reported the emergency—would get to the victim with the necessary equipment, give first aid and cold protection, and bring the person down to a lodge, shelter, or other secure point. The support team would assist the rescue team in every possible way, carrying extra food and equipment, relieving tired rescue-party members, and keeping in touch with the rescue party by radio.

To avoid delay, an advance party would leave as soon as possible; the remainder of the rescue party and the support party would follow later. Each party would have six people, and, depending on the situation, the rescue team would have at least three with technical climbing ability.

Equipment would consist of the following:

Advance Rescue Party

Sleeping bag, with full-length zipper if possible
First-aid equipment
Carrier—Basket litter, toboggan or pulk, plus rope for lashing injured person securely
Radio (two-way)
Individual equipment, including ice ax, snowshoes, crampons if necessary, food (including hot drink in vacuum bottle)
Piton hammer, pitons, carabiners, ice screws, one belay rope (if technical climbing is involved)

Support Party

Individual equipment (see above)
Radio (if not operating as a unit)

(Members of the Onondaga chapter of the Adirondack Mountain Club and its S & R leader, John Yuill, have experimented with different types of litters and have concluded that the basket litter, such as the Stokes, is the most suitable for their purposes. Fig. 95 shows a similar type of basket litter.)

When the rescue party with the carrier reaches the victim, insulation is first placed on it. Then the victim is secured on the carrier with rope so that he will not fall off. In all this, consideration is given to possible aggravation of the injury.

The injured one's head should be at the uphill end of the carrier, depending on the nature of the injuries. If the carrier is moved on the snow surface, the rear people in the party have the job of holding and controlling the carrier's progress downslope while the front people keep it on course using lines, poles, or both. Two or more additional people provide support and replacements. In steep, rocky gullies along the trail it may be necessary to use everyone available to lift the entire carrier to a point where towing or sliding downhill can be safely resumed. Ultimately a heated shelter is reached.

This type of rescue has, to a large extent, been replaced by the helicopter. The basket litter would be brought to an evacuation site or the accident site by the craft. From the evacuation site the litter would probably have to be hand carried by a ground rescue team or the helicopter rescue team to the victim. The victim then would be brought back to the helicopter by the rescue team, probably over very rough ground. This method, in distinct contrast to evacuation over ground, allows the victim to be transported with as little body disturbance as possible and in maximum comfort and safety.

A two-ski sled (Fig. 94) can be improvised from one pair of skis, one or two pairs of ski poles, three crosspieces, two leather straps, and sufficient rope for lashing and for the interlacing between the skis to support the victim. Instead of the rope interlacing and crosspieces, the victim's snowshoes could be used.

To make the sled, lash 1½ ft.-long crosspieces between the skis, spaced 8 in. apart, using the straps for the centerpiece and lines at the ski tips and heels. The ski tips should have holes bored in them to secure the line. Fasten one or two pairs of ski poles lengthwise to the crosspieces over each ski. If one pair is used, a strong fore-and-aft line has to be extended to the front crosspiece. Rig the diamond-shaped lacing, with a twist in the center, between the poles. Fasten a guide line to the rear crosspiece and a tow pole to the center of the crosspiece.

180 FINDING POSITION AND DIRECTIONS

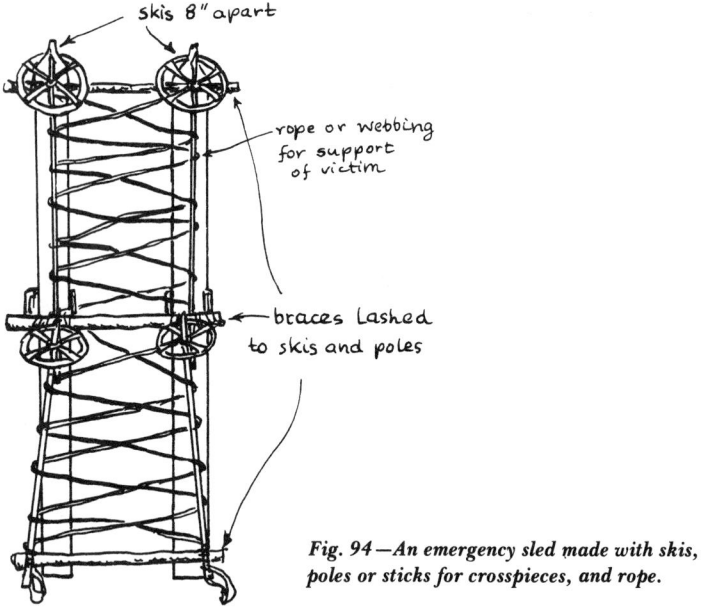

Fig. 94 — An emergency sled made with skis, poles or sticks for crosspieces, and rope.

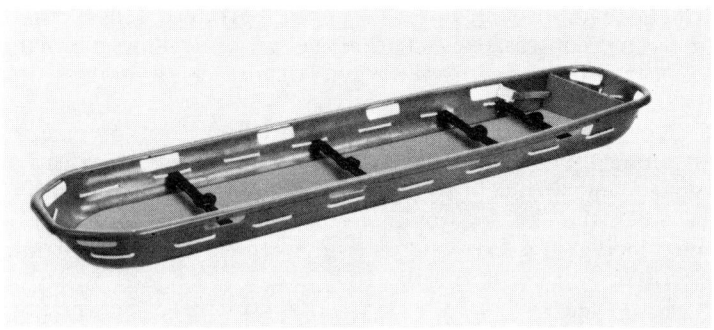

Fig. 95 — Rescue basket-sled.

This sled can be operated by two people. Unless one has had training beforehand in constructing a durable sled (one that will not fall apart on the trail with the victim on it), it is better to await the arrival of the rescue team with better equipment.

FINDING POSITION AND DIRECTIONS   181

These directions may help in an emergency. They suggest the difficulties of bringing someone out. Complications may include assembly of an evacuation party, lack of communications and proper equipment, bad weather, deep fresh snow, extreme cold, and distance to victim. Rescue procedures for all situations cannot be detailed completely. Good judgment is vital to the best possible use of available personnel and equipment.

Check your party whenever you are about to start a trip. What would you do if one of your group were injured on or near a summit with the temperature 30 below?

Evacuating injured hiker on a Stokes litter in the Adirondacks (simulated).

CASUALTY REPORTS—WHAT CAN HAPPEN

The following summaries of reported cases were randomly selected to emphasize what can happen on a winter trip, or under winter conditions, because of ignorance in general, lack of planning, inappropriate clothing, unfamiliarity with the terrain, and other causes and combinations of causes. The names are fictitious.

Case 1

Inexperienced hiker invited without knowledge of leader.
Hiking party dispersed.
Inexperienced and tired hiker left alone enroute.
Too many inexperienced hikers in party.
Failure to recognize and treat hypothermia.
RESULT: Hiker slipped and fell 500 feet, was badly injured, and required evacuation by snow vehicle and hospital treatment.

A hiking party attempted in March to climb Mount Washington via Lion's Head. Two of the group invited a friend, Albert, inexperienced and unfamiliar with the use of the ice ax and crampons, to participate—without the knowledge of the leader. Near the summit of the mountain, Albert was unable to continue the climb. The leader told him to sit on a boulder and wait for the group to return from the summit. The two that had invited Albert left the party to walk down the Auto Road, again without the knowledge of the leader. The leader then split the remaining party, some to hike down the Auto Road, he and one other to return to pick up Albert at the boulder. On reaching Albert, they found him to be cold and his reactions slow—signs of hypothermia. On hiking down the icy summit a short distance, Albert slipped and fell 500 feet down the summit to the flat area below it. With fractured knee, broken fingers, and lots of bruises, he was taken to the local hospital after evacuation by snow vehicle.

Case 2

Improper footwear.
Unfamiliarity with the trail and the time required.
Lack of sleep and food.

FINDING POSITION AND DIRECTIONS   183

Lack of trip planning.
RESULT: Three members of ski touring party developed frostbite in their feet and had to be evacuated on litters.

Eight members of a ski party arrived in New Hampshire in December to ski up to the Zealand Falls Hut via the Ethan Pond Trail. Under the impression that the trip for novice skiers would take just four hours, they began the trip at about 3 p.m. They had not had much to eat. After going about a mile, with some in the party hiking in the snow in touring boots, they made camp for the night in tents. Bob, who had been hiking, had cold feet. One stove would not operate. On continuing up the trail the next day, Barbara became cold, and the group stopped to warm her. It was then learned she had left her pack behind on the trail. At 3 p.m. the party split up: three returned to retrieve the pack, and five continued on to the hut. The retrieving group later caught up with the five on the way to the hut. When the group came to the icy slope of White Wall in Zealand Notch, some continued to the hut and one stayed behind to ensure the others' safe passage across the icy slope. Eventually the "safe man" became the last man in the approach to the hut. When the group reached the hut, it was discovered that three members had frostbitten feet. During the trip, cold sensation in the feet had stopped, and they assumed that warmth had returned when actually their feet at that point had become frozen. The three were carried out on litters.

Case 3

Only two hikers in the party.
Improper boots.
Snowshoe lost in a drift.
Failure to administer first-aid.
Leaving the victim.
RESULT: With panic possibly contributing, one member developed frostbite in the feet and required an exhausting evacuation by a rescue team.

It was December. Charles and Edward were camped at Edmonds Col in the Presidentials after having encountered severe winds and subzero temperatures while attempting to descend into trailless Jefferson Ravine. Travel had been exceptionally difficult; at one point Edward had lost a snowshoe in a drift. In camp Charles became concerned about frostbitten feet (he had been wearing hiking boots and supergaiters). They decided that Edward should get help at Pinkham Notch, which he eventually reached that evening. A rescue group finally reached the camp via snow vehicle up the Auto Road. The report stated "the evacuation was one of the most exhausting in recent years." Charles was treated for frostbite at the local hospital.

Case 4

Only two hikers in the party.
Improper clothing.
No previous winter training or experience.
Leaving victim without giving first-aid.
RESULT: Victim was severely hypothermic, and was dead on arrival at the ranger station.

In November David and Joseph went to the Adirondacks to backpack in the High Peak area, entering in the vicinity of Newcomb. It was David's first backpacking experience. He wore waffle-type cotton drawers, blue jeans, a cotton flannel shirt, heavy wool socks, and summer hiking boots. Joseph's clothing was similar except for corduroy knickers. Snow was on the ground; temperature was in the low 20's; there were snow flurries. The plan was to hike from Lake Henderson to Lake Colden and spend the night there. In the approach to the lake and in the area between Clinton and Iroquois it was almost dark, with up to 18 inches of snow on unbroken trail. In the pass area, David lagged behind and started to show signs of hypothermia, which were not noticed. After a short rest and a snack, he resumed hiking but began to stumble and often fell in the snow. He wanted to stop, but Joseph wanted to keep moving. David fell twice in a brook, got his legs wet, and shortly thereafter was unable to walk. When about a half mile from the ranger station at Lake Colden, Joseph went ahead for help. Before leaving he put his down jacket on David. Both had lost their caps. David's pack with a down jacket, sleeping bag, and pad were beside him, untouched. Joseph reached the station at about 7 p.m. At about 8:30 p.m. a rescue team, including Joseph and three hikers, left the station with hot tea, a lantern, and a rescue sled. Temperature was 16°F, wind up to 10 mph. When the group reached David about 45 minutes later, they found him barely conscious, unable to walk, and with a shallow pulse. They gave him tea, wrapped him in his sleeping bag, and put him in the sled. About 15 minutes from the ranger station, David's breathing had stopped, and he had no detectable pulse. On reaching the station, David's heart had stopped beating. He could not be revived by massage and mouth-to-mouth breathing. David was dead.

Case 5

Insufficient liquid intake, resulting in dehydration.
Sucking on icicle to quench thirst.
Possible consumption of alcohol the preceding night.
RESULT: Hiker developed stomach cramps, felt severely ill, and had to be given first-aid. A rescue team evacuated him to a hut where his body heat and general physical condition were restored. First-aid actions probably prevented a worse result.

In October a group of hikers left to climb Franconia Ridge. Temperatures were in the 20's; maximum wind speed was at least 30 mph; rain and snow were falling; snow covered the rocks in the ridge. The group pushed to reach the summit by noon. Samuel felt extremely thirsty on the way, having had just one cup of cocoa that morning, so on the way he sucked on an icicle. In the vicinity of the summit of Lincoln, Samuel experienced violent stomach cramps and began to vomit. The group stopped and set up a tent on the lee side of the ridge and sent for help at the Greenleaf Hut, about 2 miles away. When Samuel was put into a sleeping bag with a companion, his condition stabilized. A rescue group of hut people and hikers along the trail was formed. Samuel was carried by litter across the ridge to the hut. During the trip, he suffered greatly. In the hut he was put into a sleeping bag with another hiker and given warm drinks. Later, he recovered sufficiently to eat some food. In the morning Samuel was well enough to walk out.

Mountain Weather

IN ANTICIPATION of any winter trip your first obligation is to get information on the weather and climatic extremes. How cold does it get? How windy? Will you need crampons?

The solution, as every experienced hiker knows, boils down to this simple imperative: Be Prepared—that is, have a good idea of the *worst* conditions that could be encountered on the trip and be adequately equipped for the temperature, wind, and snow and ice extremes. If one does not know what the worst conditions might be, at least one should try to get the information by asking others. Not having enough clothing or the necessary shell parka, or having improper handwear, the wrong kind of hat, or inadequate boots can ruin a trip. It ends up being a hardship instead of enjoyed as it could have been. Safety, too, is jeopardized.

By being prepared for the worst, one does not have to be entirely dependent on getting a weather forecast before embarking on a trip. If the weather during the trip becomes intolerable, or is expected to be, one always has the option of aborting.

The following comments and data were developed to give the reader some notion of the weather and climate in the mountain areas of New York and New England.

SOME INFLUENCES OF MOUNTAINS ON WEATHER

Generally mountains influence local weather by encouraging cloud formation, increasing precipitation, and tending to make winds variable and turbulent.

Cloud Formation

When air moving along the earth's surface reaches a mountain, it moves upward and expands as the atmospheric pressure decreases. In expanding it cools, usually below its dewpoint (temperature at which the air is saturated with moisture in the form of vapor). Therefore some of its moisture condenses out to form clouds and perhaps precipitation. This so-called adiabatic cooling will produce clouds beginning at the level

MOUNTAIN WEATHER 187

The Presidentials offer weather in many moods. The view here is from Mt. Success.

where the dewpoint is reached. More clouds may form at higher altitudes, depending on the relative humidity, elevation, and other factors. Clouds that are formed locally in this way are of a common type.

Passing over the summit or ridge to the leeward side, the air moves downward. Now it compresses and heats up, and its capacity to contain moisture as vapor increases. Clouds in this air begin to evaporate.

Thus mountain terrain favors cloud formation, often on the windward side of slopes and below summits. The formation, movement, and destruction of clouds in a mountain system are, of course, highly complex phenomena.

Precipitation

Rain: When upper air above a temperature of about 10°F condenses, it produces clouds. As these become denser, tiny buoyant droplets tend to coalesce to form drops, which if large enough—1/125 in. or larger—fall as rain.

Snow: Ice crystals in the form of snowflakes are formed when moisture condenses from supersaturated air (air saturated beyond its normal water-holding capacity) at temperatures below about 10°F. The common saying that "it's too cold to snow" is inaccurate, though it is true that snow is more common at higher temperatures. Snow has fallen in Alaska at −52°F.

At very low temperatures snow is likely to be very light "powder." New, fluffy, dry snow contains about 97 per cent entrapped air, which provides much insulation. Snow does not absorb much heat during the day and it cools rapidly at night. It reflects about 75% of sunlight, absorbs about 25%.

Pellet snow (graupel), which is granular, is formed by the accumulation of a rime (frozen moisture) deposit on falling snow crystals. The crystals develop into rounded balls.

Fallen snow builds up in layers, is compacted, may melt somewhat, and gradually loses its crystalline character, becoming rounded grains called old snow, or névé. Pressure and temperature are important in this process.

The National Weather Service has to be consistent in its use of terms. These have the following senses in snow warnings:

"snow"
> A regular downfall, but the term can be modified by "occasional" or "intermittent."

"heavy snow"
> Four or more inches are anticipated in the following 12 hours, 6 or more in the following 24 hours.

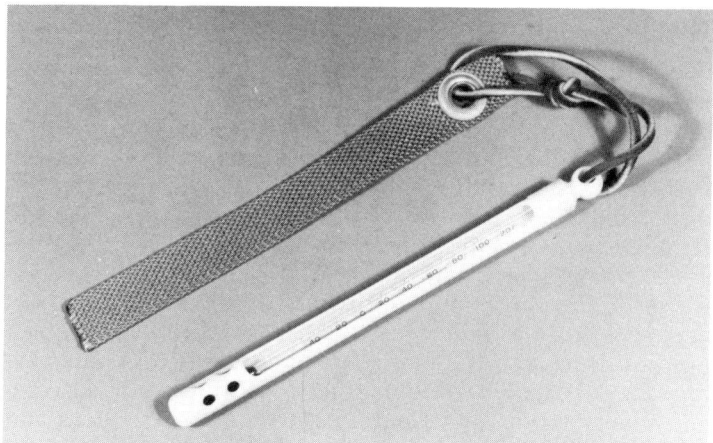

Fig. 96—Minimum thermometer.

"snow flurries"
Visibility may be impaired during intermittent snowfall.
"snow squalls"
Short and heavy snowfalls with strong winds.
"blizzard"
Snowfall with winds 35 mph or more and temperatures 20°F or lower for a long period.
"severe blizzard"
Dense snow with visibility almost nil, winds 45 mph or more, and temperatures 10°F or lower.

Hail: This falls only in connection with thunderstorms (which do sometimes occur in winter). A hailstone consists of a water droplet that has acquired one or more coatings of ice by being carried up and down by air currents through one or more subfreezing air layers. Successive coatings may form an onionlike structure.

Sleet: This consists of small particles of clear ice. These originally formed as raindrops but froze as they fell through a cold air layer. Some people use the term "sleet" also for a mixture of rain and snow, or for partly melted snow.

Weather men apply the term *glaze* to supercooled raindrops which freeze upon striking the ground or other surfaces. Glaze gives us what is popularly termed an "ice storm." Deposits of 2 in. or more have been recorded.

Winds

Because of differences in temperature between air at higher altitudes and lower altitudes, there are usually convectional air movements on a slope.

Generally, the higher one gets on a mountain, the more noticeable is the wind. When planning an ascent, especially in winter, one must take account of the probability that wind will be much greater on the summit than below. And above timberline sheltered places may not exist.

During the day, mountain surfaces usually warm up faster than valleys; the mountain air thus becomes lighter and moves upward. During the night the mountains lose heat faster than the valleys, so that the mountain air is cooled, becomes heavier, and moves downslope. Cold air accumulates in valleys and other low-elevation pockets. Thus the temperature in such places may be lower than at points on the mountain. Convectional air currents of this kind produce "valley breezes."

MICROCLIMATE

Temperature and wind conditions encountered depend on factors such as the kind of trail, amount of snow, whether one is above the treeline, and kind of shelter. The sum total of weather characteristics in a particular place is called a "microclimate." Some understanding of microclimates may reduce apprehension about winter camping and is particularly important in survival.

If it is windy at a low elevation, surely a gale is blowing on the summit. If wind velocity is more than 45 mph there, one can expect extreme difficulty in trying to move about. Gusts may reach 100 mph, so that you may have to crawl to get to the top. Under these circumstances people have managed to reach the summit and return safely, but one must use caution and good judgment before undertaking any such effort. Rather than take unnecessary risks, turn back.

Wind speed can be estimated by observing the wind's effects on smoke, branches, and tree tops. See Table 15.

In approaching a summit you will be hiking along a trail below treeline, generally through forest cover. Most of the wind force is absorbed by the crowns of the trees—where most of the branches are located. But in open spaces the wind will

TABLE 15

Beaufort Scale

Force No.	Designation	Velocity, mph	Observable Effects
0	Calm	Less than 1	Smoke rises vertically
1	Light air	1–3	Direction of wind shown by smoke drift, but not by wind vanes
2	Slight breeze	4–7	Wind felt on face; ordinary vane moved by wind
3	Gentle breeze	8–12	Large and small twigs in constant motion
4	Moderate breeze	13–18	Small branches are moved
5	Fresh breeze	19–24	Small trees begin to sway
6	Strong breeze	25–31	Large branches in motion
7	Moderate gale	32–38	Whole trees in motion; inconvenience felt in walking against the wind
8	Fresh gale	39–46	Breaks twigs off trees, generally impedes progress
9	Strong gale	47–54	Common on summits; breaks branches; walking more difficult—may have to crawl

swirl down on you. More wind will reach the ground as forest growth shortens near the treeline. On the windward side of an overlook or gully you will begin to feel the full wind force. At the treeline, in some spot sheltered from the wind, one should prepare for the worst by putting on extra clothing, face mask, crampons, or other needed equipment. Hands, face, and any other exposed flesh must be protected from the effects of wind-chill.

Within a snow cover, tent, or emergency shelter the winter mountaineer is exposed to certain temperature differences, intentionally or otherwise. Table 16 indicates the relative warmth actually provided by a snow shelter under changing conditions. These points should be noted: (1) big difference between outside and inside temperature; (2) increase in inside temperature due to door, candles, or body heat.

The temperature gradient with snow cover can vary considerably. The ground surface underneath the cover contains heat, which is conserved by the insulating snow layer. In one test the air temperature 3 ft. above the snow surface was $-40°F$,

TABLE 16
Relative Warmth Provided by a Snow Shelter[36]

Temperature (°F)			
Outside	Inside	Situation	Time
−17	18*	Unoccupied	3:30 p.m.
−36	20*	Unoccupied	8:15 a.m.
−40	21*	Unoccupied	8:00 a.m.
−36	19*	Unoccupied	8:00 a.m.
−12	16*	Unoccupied	4:30 p.m.
− 2	7	Occupied, no door, unoccupied several hours	
− 7	14	Door in place, occupied, not occupied at time of reading, no heat	
−48	23.5	2 occupants, 2 candles for 15 minutes	
−55	19	2 occupants overnight, no heat	

*During these recordings the temperature of the ground surface underneath undisturbed snow was 14° to 19°F.

but the ground temperature was 19°F. Because of heat in the ground a thin layer of the initial snowfall is melted during the course of the winter. The temperature of this layer tends to be about 32°F.

WEATHER IN THE ADIRONDACKS AND THE WHITE MOUNTAINS

Mountains in the Northeast are essentially oversized, heavily wooded hills, with occasional bare rock summits. Some peaks in the Adirondacks of New York and in the White Mountains of New Hampshire reach 5,000 ft. or more and have a timberline at around 4,500 to 5,000 ft., above which no sizeable vegetation grows. Winter weather in these areas is severe and highly variable as to both elevation and time.

The wind, when generally light at low elevations, may exceed 75 mph on the mountain tops. On the summit of Mt. Washington the probability of hurricane-force wind (75 mph or more) is about 58%.

Temperature may drop as much as 5° per 1,000 ft. of rise, but sometimes there is little difference between low- and high-elevation temperatures. On some occasions the temperature on the upper reaches of a mountain is higher than at lower elevations. Once when the temperature on the summit of Mt. Washington was 30°F, Pinkham Notch recorded −1.2°F. In general, a normal temperature range within a few days is 30°F to −10°F, but it may be 40°F to −30°F. A range of 30°F to −30°F is common.

Precipitation of measurable quantity—that is, 0.1 in. or more of snow—will occur on about half of the days, 1 in. or more on about a quarter of the days, and rain on about a tenth or less of the days.

It can and often does rain on the mountains at unexpected times and elevations. Rain may fall at below-freezing temperatures, freezing on contact wherever it lands. After the rain ceases, the temperature usually drops 20° to 30° or more within the next 24 hours.

Starting in November, a layer of snow or ice, or both, covers the ground. Snow depth will increase until March. Depth varies widely. There has been as much as 100 ft. of drift snow in Tuckerman Ravine on Mt. Washington.

Generally, in the mountains there is often as much as 200 in. Exposed areas and steep slopes generally have a comparatively thin covering — mostly ice. Sheltered areas usually acquire several times the average depth of soft snow. Other conditions being equal, snow depth increases with elevation by at least 1 ft. per 1,000 ft. of rise. Over a 40-year period the average annual snowfall in the region of the White Mountains and the Adirondacks was about 80 in.

Tables 17 to 19 here give the essential weather data for Mt. Washington and Pinkham Notch in the White Mountains. This data indicates the severe weather conditions for which a winter party should be prepared. Mountains lower than Mt. Washington will have less severe weather.

TABLE 17
Average Number of Days with 75-mph or Greater Wind on Mt. Washington

December	18
January	19
February	15
March	21
April	15

194 MOUNTAIN WEATHER

In Tuckerman Ravine on Mt. Washington.

TABLE 18
Probability of Days with 1/10 inch or More of Precipitation in the White Mountains

Elevation (feet)	Probability
380	42%
620	38
950	40
1,870	50
4,870	49
6,288	59

TABLE 19
Weather Data for Mt. Washington and Pinkham Notch

	Dec.	Jan.	Feb.	Mar.
Summit of Mount Washington (6,288 ft.)				
Temperature—record minimum—°F	−46	−46	−46	−38
Snowfall—mean, inches	27	27	24	26
Snowfall—maximum, inches	49	48	45	44
Wind speed—average, mph	48	50	49	46
Days with fog—7 a.m., mean	16	14	15	17
Pinkham Notch (2,000 ft.)				
Temperature—recorded minimum −°F	−32	−28	−32	−21
Snowfall—mean, inches	27	35	30	33
Snowfall—maximum, inches	48	64	44	61

On Mt. Washington the most severe storms are usually from the southwest. Prevailing winds are west and west-northwest. On April 12, 1934, a wind gust on Mt. Washington reached a record 231 mph!

The Adirondacks and White Mountains are, emphatically, areas of extreme cold and high winds in winter. The climatic extremes there, at about 44° north latitude, are equal to polar conditions. "With the exception of some isolated peaks in the Arctic and Antarctic, Mt. Washington has the most severe weather in the world," said Bradford Washburn. The Great Lakes and Canada are the sources of the cold prevailing winds. On reaching the beginning of the White Mountains in the west, these winds speed at modest rates but of course in huge volume. As the wind goes up the gradual west slope of Mt. Washington, that volume has to pass through and over a confined area, so that wind speed has to increase greatly. This action is roughly comparable to the increase in speed over the top of an aircraft wing.

Table 20 showing minimum temperatures in or in the vicinity of principal mountains, compiled from the U.S. National Weather Service Summary for the year 1975, may also be helpful.

Although the following data on wind speed and total snowfall is mostly from cities and towns, it may be helpful to outsiders in anticipating weather extremes in the area.

TABLE 20
Minimum Temperatures (°F)
(Reports from weather stations in or in the vicinity of principal mountains)

1975

New York

Taconic Mountains	Grafton −14; Valatie −15; Millbrook −7
Catskill Mountains	Downsville Dam −13; Slide Mountain (base) −7, (summit, 1979) −24; Walton −15
Adirondack Mountains	Boonville −15; Gabriels −25; Indian Lake −26; Lake Placid −27; Lowville −19; Newcomb −30; Old Forge −30; Speculator −25; Stillwater Reservoir −24; Tupper Lake −25; Wanakena Ranger School −29

Connecticut

Taconic Mountains	Falls Village −12

Massachusetts

Berkshire Hills	Borden Brook Reservoir −11; Chester −20; Hoosac Tunnel −10; Knightsville Dam −10; Shelburne Falls −10; Cummington Hill −9
Taconic Mountains	Adams −10; Lanesboro −14; Stockbridge −12

Vermont

Green Mountains	Chelsea −25; Montpelier −14; Northfield −25; Rochester −26; Waterbury −22; Bristol −19; Burlington −16; Rutland −14; Ball Mountain Lake −20; Bellows Falls −11; Cavendish −23; Readsboro −15

New Hampshire

White Mountains	Mt. Washington −32; Pinkham Notch −27; Benton −18; Bethlehem −19; Woodstock −18
North Country	Berlin −18; Colebrook −31; First Connecticut Lake −33; Lancaster −26; North Stratford −30
Monadnocks	Franklin Falls Dam −23; Hanover −17; Keene −16; Lebanon −20; Mt. Sunapee −15; Peterboro −13; Plymouth −18; Surry Mountain Lake −20

Maine

White Mountains	Greenville −19; Rangeley −30; Long Falls Dam −24
Katahdin Mountains	Ripogenus Dam −26; Millinocket −22; Patten −24

TABLE 21

Total Snowfall and Maximum Wind Speed

1974

	Total Snowfall (in.)	Wind Speed (max.)	
		mph	Direction
New York			
Albany	55	46	NW
Binghamton	79	40	W
Buffalo	110	50	W
Rochester	105	45	SW
Syracuse	114	59	W
Connecticut			
Hartford	37	41	NW
Massachusetts			
Blue Hill Obs.	47	70	NW
Worcester	48	42	—
Vermont			
Burlington	99	47	NW
New Hampshire			
Concord	55	48	NW
Mt. Washington Obs.	368*	137	SW
Maine			
Caribou	121	—	—
Portland	46	43	NW

*1973

Radio Weather Reports

Latest weather information may be obtained from National Weather Service continuous FM broadcasts on the 162.55, 162.40, and 162.475 MHz frequencies. According to the Service, broadcasts can usually be received 35 to 40 and perhaps 60 miles from the transmitting antenna site, depending on the quality of receiver used, terrain and height of antenna. Particular attention should be paid to the manufacturer's sensitivity rating of the receiver.

Taped messages are broadcast every four to six minutes and usually amended every one to three hours with the latest information. The latter may include radar summaries and detailed local and area forecasts. Routine reports may be interrupted for severe weather warnings.

Stations in the New York-New England area:
New York
  Albany, Binghamton, Buffalo, Elmira, Kingston, New York City, Rochester, Syracuse
Connecticut
  Hartford, Meriden, New London
Massachusetts
  Boston, Hyannis, Worcester
New Hampshire
  Concord
Vermont
  Burlington, Windsor
Maine
  Ellsworth, Portland

Reports from the Portland station have been received by a hiker above treeline near the summit of Mt. Washington using a small transistor radio—about one pound [48]. The hiker stated further that "The reception from Portland has always been clear on peaks of 4,000 feet and up, and in many instances (such as Zealand Hut) I could pick up the weathercast on eastward facing slopes down to as low as 3,000 feet."

Winter Storms

According to the National Weather Service[49], winter storms "are generated, as are many of the thunderstorms of summer, from disturbances along the boundary between cold polar and warm tropical air masses, the fronts where air masses of different temperatures and densities wage their perpetual war of instability and equilibrium. The disturbances may become intense low-pressure systems, churning over tens of thousands of square miles in a great counterclockwise sweep.

"On our east coast, winter storms often form along the Atlantic polar front near the coast of Virginia and the Carolinas and in the general area east of the southern Appalachians. These are the notorious Cape Hatteras storms—nor'easters—which develop in great intensity as they move up the coast, then drift seaward toward Iceland, where they finally decay.

"Because they form over water, these storms are difficut to forecast, and occasionally surprise the Atlantic megalopolis with paralyzing snows. In 1969, the U.S. Departments of Commerce, Transportation, and Defense tightened winter storm surveillance by adding reconnaissance aircraft, an ocean buoy, and a new weather ship. With better hour-to-hour information on the storms, weathermen ashore have begun to ease the burden of unexpected heavy snows in eastern cities."

The National Weather Service uses the terms "watch" and "warning" in their reports. "The 'watch' alerts the public that a storm has formed and is approaching the area. People in the alerted area should keep listening for the latest advisories over radio and television, and begin to take precautionary measures. The 'warning' means that a storm is imminent and immediate action should be taken to protect life and property."

In the Adirondacks: Mt. Marcy from Phelps.

You and the Environment

HIKERS SHOULD BE PROUD of the fact that they have been and continue to be pioneers and leaders in the conservation movement. Their obvious proximity to the land was supremely advantageous to the task—slowly and step by step, eyes scanning the horizon and the trail, absorbing and thinking about the significance of it all, asking questions, organizing, getting legislation passed, preventing unwise development and senseless exploitation, preserving and protecting natural open spaces and features. "Conservation" was the watchword, largely replaced today by "ecology"—signifying interaction of plant and animal life in a particular environment, an ecosystem. Serious awareness, too, that Man is a part of the system and that his future in the environment is in peril. No longer is he considered the being supreme, not subject to natural laws.

WITH RESPECT TO TRAILS, A MAJOR ENVIRONMENTAL CONCERN IS THE HIKER HIMSELF

In recent years hikers and their clubs have put increased emphasis on protecting and preserving the trail and its natural setting. They have intensively studied, discussed and asked questions about trail use and deteriorating influences: the impact of large numbers of hikers, carrying capacity, recreational vehicles, nonreturnable containers, noise pollution, vandalism, trail facilities, soil compaction, overuse, erosion, trail education, trail relocation, permit and caretaker systems, and trail patrols.

In response to an inquiry regarding the impact of hikers and campers on the winter environment, Dr. E. H. Ketchledge of the State University of New York College of Environmental Science and Forestry said:

"I do not know of any detailed, specific studies on the environmental impact of hikers and skiers during the winter season. My own observations, however, are:

"1. At lower elevations when the ground is frozen and covered with snow, there is essentially no unusual, out-of-the-ordinary impact when camping is discrete. By that I mean if a gas stove is used instead of a campfire, if no vegetation is damaged in putting up the tent, if litter is removed, if human waste is deposited a goodly distance off in the woods away from traffic.

"2. The probability of damage increases sharply at the higher elevations and above timberline is so critical that it should be prohibited.... The alpine ecosystem is just as protected by ice and snow as the lower, forested areas during mid-winter BUT the *start* of the winter season and the *end* of the winter season are the two most critical periods in the annual cycle.

"At the start of the season, when the alpine meadow is beginning to freeze up (a period extending with interruptions and reversals from September into December) but is not yet covered with a protective blanket of ice and snow, any trespass over the *vegetation* crushes the brittle plant tissues; footprints become in fact lasting, three-dimensional prints of the foot, not simply ephemeral images of where a foot once pressed down on a springy, rebounding vegetational cover.

"In the spring it is particularly the *soil* which is damaged, for as the ground unfreezes, the black, organic soil that constitutes these alpine situations becomes as wet and soggy and weak as that of any lowland bog; the hiker actually sinks into the soil as he walks upon the meadow, this time tearing apart the root systems of the fragile plants as well as inflicting damage on the aerial parts.

"Because these two critical periods—when actual survival of the ecosystem is at stake—immediately interface at either end with the deep-winter season, that is, start and finish of 'the winter,' and because the timing of that ecologically critical period shifts (and repeats!) from year to year, we have no choice but to urge NO CAMPING on the summits whatsoever, even though you and I and other ecologically sensitive recreationists know there are a few weeks in mid-winter when summit camping could be accomplished by *qualified* campers. It is unreasonable to expect the average camper to perceive these critical subtleties or to be aware when they exist. Moreover, camping on the summits for most hikers is a stress period, a period of challenge; that in part is what brings them there. And I have seen for a fact, during such stress situations all but the most disciplined mountaineer will relax his standards on picking up litter, going far off in the woods to eliminate, and the like. We simply can't take such chances, then, of permitting ecologically dangerous uses of our most unique piece of natural real estate, the alpine summits.

"My basic fear about camping problems in general is that we keep talking about responsible woodsmanship and what we should and should not do, and in the long run these efforts will pay off with a higher sense of stewardship toward the land. Yet there will always be ecological crimes committed on the landscape by the small percentage of hikers who escape our educational efforts. In the case of selected, high-value recreational spots such as the alpine summits, our only assurance of preserving the resource is to prohibit potentially destructive activities. That is the compromise we must reach with the natural environment if we are to use it without destroying it, which is the creed of all conservationalists. In this case, that means it is OK to walk across the well-managed trail over a summit and to enjoy its vista and observe its fauna and flora but *not to camp upon it*."

To deal with the most urgent problems—littering and abuse at convenient access points, destruction of shelters, disturbance of wildlife, destruction of plant life, vandalism and littering at shelters and campsites—new emphasis was put on trail education, paid or volunteer trail patrols were organized and put into operation, and written codes of trail ethics were introduced.

These efforts were aimed at modifying and influencing trail behavior through direct personal contact and low-key, informal education. Simply put, it's a matter of developing a personal association or feeling about the trail and environment and imparting this to others. This is an enormous task that will take years to accomplish noticeable improvements. To make any significant dent in the problems, efforts must be continuous. Every hiker must be involved.

In his essay on the Conservation Esthetic, Aldo Leopold said, "To promote perception is the only truly creative part of recreational engineering. This fact is important and its potential power for bettering 'the good life' is only dimly understood.... Let no man jump to the conclusion that Babbitt must take his Ph.D. in ecology before he can 'see' his country."

Improving hikers' concern, understanding, awareness, or consciousness under a set of operating principles would do much toward protecting and preserving the environment.

A PERSONAL CODE, written from the standpoint of this book, was developed for your consideration:

- To preserve plant and animal life and natural features so that they may be enjoyed to the fullest now and in the future.
- To observe, but not to disturb, any animals that may be encountered.
- To be especially aware that mountain summits above treeline contain fragile plant communities, and in this respect to know about special limitations — the restrictions against camping above the 4,000 foot level in the Adirondacks and above treeline in the White Mountains.
- To carry out all left-over food and containers; to leave nothing behind at a shelter, campsite, or other stopping point. This means taking refuse home (preferably) or to a waste container that *you know* is emptied regularly.
- To have a litter bag in the pack at all times for refuse.

    (Every hiker must be aware of the tremendous amounts of garbage and litter left at shelters, campsites, scenic spots and picnic areas during non-winter months by thoughtless and indifferent people, many of whom, especially during summer months at convenient access points to trails, are not hikers. Although winter hiking is done by relatively few, the weather, extreme cold, and inexperience can easily result in damaged or cheap equipment, garbage, and packaging left at the campsite or shelter. All such items, including paper, plastic, and aluminum foil, must be brought out. No flammable refuse, or supposedly flammable, should be burned at a fireplace or campsite.)
- To clean any utensils away from, not in, streams or other water sources; to use biodegradable soap.
- To limit a group's size to the number which can be effectively managed and led by a single leader. Upon using your judgment about the particular conditions and type of trip, the ratio should be less than the maximum of eight.
- To be aware that human waste is a special problem where there is no facility. Walk or ski off the trail to eliminate, and at a considerable distance from any camping area or water source.
- Standing timber, whether live, dead or apparently dead, and boughs shall not be cut for fire or shelter construction. Leave the ax at home. Your winter skill and know-how is shown by

independence from the wood fire. Instead use a stove or the other methods cited for increasing warmth.
- Finally, to check the campsite or shelter before you leave and ask yourself:

    WHAT EFFECT ON THE ENVIRONMENT DID MY PRESENCE AND ACTIVITY HAVE?
    DID I DAMAGE IT, OR DID I PRESERVE AND PROTECT IT?

To help you learn more about winter natural history and ecology, a list of articles and books on the subject has been compiled. See the Appendix.

Appendix

GLOSSARY OF TERRAIN FEATURES

Bluff
A high, steep, broad-faced bank or cliffs
Bulge
A sharp but short increase in steepness
Buttress
Protruding portion of a rock face or ridge
Chimney
Vertical opening between masses of rock, large enough to hold body of climber
Cirque
Valley head opened up into bowl shape by glacial action
Cliff
A high, steep rock or face of rock
Col
In some areas, same as saddle; the low point in a ridge between summits
Cornice
An overhanging mass of wind-packed snow formed at the crest of a ridge
Couloir
A wide, U-shaped gully
Gendarme
A tower or pinnacle dominating a ridge and making an obstacle to progress
Gully
A steep-sided small ravine on a mountainside, often with a stream in it
Knoll
A small hill, usually somewhat rounded
Pinnacle
A slender, pointed, upright rock mass
Ravine
A steep-sided trench cut into a mountainside by running water, smaller than a valley but larger than a gully or gulch
Ridge
A long, narrow highland or group of highlands
Saddle
The part of a ridge between two peaks or summits

Slab
　A smooth, slanting rock surface
Spur
　A minor highland projecting laterally from the main mass of mountain or mountain range
Summit
　Highest point of mountain
Terrace
　A wide ledge
Trough
　A long narrow depression with a rounded cross section
U-shaped valley
　A valley with a U-shaped cross section, resulting from erosion by a glacier
Valley
　A large trench cut by a river; or, loosely, an elongated basin produced by faulting

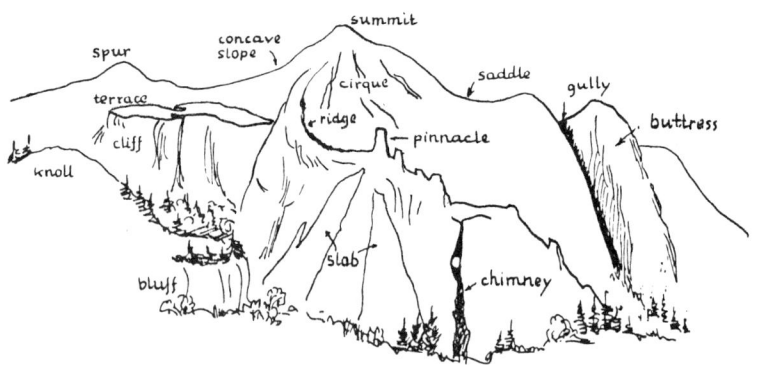

Fig. 97 — Terrain features and their names.

METRIC EQUIVALENTS

During the transition period when the U. S. is converting to the metric system, and in anticipation of the conversion, these metric equivalents will probably be helpful — in measuring distances, heights, menus, and your pack load. Often a rough calculation is all that is needed. Round the numbers according to your individual requirements.

CELSIUS-FAHRENHEIT EQUIVALENTS

U.S. Measures	Metric Units
1 oz (ounce)	28.35 g (gram)
1 lb (pound)	0.45 kg (kilogram)
1 in (inch)	2.54 cm (centimeter)
1 ft (foot)	30.48
1 yd (yard)	0.91 m (meter)
1 mi (mile)	1.61 km (kilometer)
1 sq mi (square mile)	2.59 sq km
1 pt (pint) U.S. liquid—28.88 cu in)	0.47 l (litre)
1 qt (quart) (U.S. liquid)	0.95 l
1 gal (gallon) U.S. liquid—231 cu in)	3.79 l

LOW TEMPERATURE
CELSIUS—FAHRENHEIT EQUIVALENTS

°C	°F
2	35.6
0	32.0
− 2	28.4
− 4	24.8
− 6	21.2
− 8	17.6
−10	14.0
−12	10.4
−14	6.8
−16	3.2
−18	0.4
−20	− 4.0
−22	− 7.6
−24	−11.2
−26	−14.8
−28	−18.4
−30	−22.0
−32	−25.6
−34	−29.2
−36	−32.8
−38	−36.4
−40	−40.0

Formula for converting from Celsius to Fahrenheit scale: Multiply Celsius temperature by 2, substract 10%, then add 32.

HIGH PEAKS OF THE NORTHEASTERN UNITED STATES

NEW YORK
Adirondacks

Mountain	Elev., m.	Elev., ft.	Mountain	Elev., m.	Elev., ft.
Marcy	1,629	5,344	Allen	1,323	4,340
Algonquin	1,559	5,114	Big Slide	1,292	4,240
Haystack	1,512	4,960	Esther	1,292	4,240
Skylight	1,501	4,926	Upper Wolfjaw	1,276	4,185
Whiteface	1,483	4,867	Lower Wolfjaw	1,273	4,175
Dix	1,480	4,857	Street	1,270	4,166
Gray Peak	1,475	4,840	Phelps	1,268	4,161
Iroquois	1,475	4,840	Donaldson	1,262	4,140
Basin	1,471	4,827	Seymour	1,256	4,120
Gothics	1,444	4,736	Sawteeth	1,250	4,100
Colden	1,437	4,714	Cascade	1,249	4,098
Giant	1,410	4,627	South Dix	1,237	4,060
Nippletop	1,408	4,620	Porter	1,237	4,059
Santanoni	1,404	4,607	Colvin	1,237	4,057
Redfield	1,404	4,606	Emmons	1,231	4,040
Wright	1,396	4,580	Street, W. Summit	1,230	4,034
Saddleback	1,376	4,515	Dial	1,225	4,020
Panther	1,354	4,442	Yard	1,225	4,018
Table Top	1,349	4,427	East Dix	1,223	4,012
Rocky Peak	1,347	4,420	MacNaughton	1,219	4,000
Macomb	1,343	4,405	Blake	1,207	3,960
Armstrong	1,341	4,400	Cliff	1,207	3,960
Hough	1,341	4,400	Nye	1,187	3,895
Seward	1,329	4,361	Couchsachraga	1,164	3,820
Marshall	1,329	4,360			

Catskills

Mountain	Elev., m.	Elev., ft.	Mountain	Elev., m.	Elev., ft.
Slide	1,274	4,180	Friday	1,126	3,694
Hunter	1,231	4,040	Big Indian	1,122	3,680
Black Dome	1,216	3,990	Rusk	1,122	3,680
Thomas Cole	1,202	3,945	High Peak	1,114	3,655
Blackhead	1,201	3,940	Twin	1,109	3,640
Westkill	1,183	3,880	Fir	1,105	3,625
Doubletop	1,180	3,870	Balsam Cap	1,104	3,623
Graham	1,179	3,868	North Dome	1,100	3,610
Cornell	1,178	3,865	Eagle	1,098	3,605
Table	1,173	3,847	Balsam	1,097	3,600
Peekamoose	1,171	3,843	Bearpen	1,097	3,600
Plateau	1,170	3,840	Indian Head	1,089	3,573

HIGH PEAKS OF THE NORTHEAST

Sugarloaf (Mink)	1,158	3,800	Mt. Sherill	1,079	3,540
Wittenberg	1,152	3,780	Vly	1,076	3,529
Balsam Lake	1,135	3,725	Windham High Peak	1,074	3,524
Lone	1,134	3,721	Halcott	1,073	3,520
Panther	1,134	3,720	Rocky	1,069	3,508

VERMONT—Green Mountains

Mountain	Elev., m.	Elev., ft.	Moutain	Elev., m.	Elev., ft.
Mansfield	1,339	4,393	Tabor	1.092	3,584
Killington Peak	1,293	4,241	Roosevelt	1,091	3,580
Ellen	1,260	4,135	Cleveland	1,070	3,510
Camel's Hump	1,244	4,083	Ira Allen	1,069	3,506
Abraham	1,235	4,052	Styles	1,038	3,404
Lincoln	1,223	4,013	Admiral Dewey	1,027	3,371
Pico	1,209	3,967	Belvidere	1,024	3,360
Jay	1,177	3,861	Carmel	1,018	3,341
Stratton	1,170	3,839	White Rocks	1,008	3,307
Breadloaf	1,165	3,823	Worth	1,006	3,300
Glastonbury	1,147	3,764	Bromley	994	3,260
Wilson	1,145	3,756	Haystack	982	3,223
Bolton	1,135	3,725	Admiral Mayo	963	3,160
Whiteface	1.132	3,715	Horrid	957	3,140
Ethan Allen	1,124	3,688	Tillotson	927	3,040
Madonna	1,118	3,668	Admiral Clarke	908	2,979
Grant	1,116	3,661	Domey's Dome	878	2,880
General Stark	1,093	3,585	Laraway	853	2,800

NEW HAMPSHIRE—White Mountains

Mountain	Elev., m.	Elev., ft.	Mountain	Elev., m.	Elev., ft.
Washington	1,917	6,288	Osceola	1,319	4,326
Adams	1,767	5,798	Clinton	1,314	4,312
Jefferson	1,742	5,715	Willey	1,311	4,302
Monroe	1,641	5,385	Zealand	1,311	4,301
Madison	1,635	5,363	North Kinsman	1,305	4,273
Lafayette	1,600	5,249	Hancock, S. Peak	1,303	4,274
Lincoln	1,557	5,108	Osceola, E. Peak	1,276	4,185
South Twin	1,501	4,926	Cabot	1,274	4,180
Carter Dome	1,476	4,843	Tripyramid,		
Moosilauke	1,466	4,810	N. Peak	1,262	4,140
North Twin	1,454	4,769	Middle Peak	1,253	4,110
Pleasant	1,451	4,761	Cannon	1,243	4,077
Bond	1,437	4,714	Hale	1,243	4,077
Carrigain	1,426	4,680	Passaconaway	1,237	4,060
Middle Carter	1,408	4,621	Jackson	1,235	4,052
Bond, West Peak	1,380	4,526	Tom	1,234	4,047
Garfield	1,368	4,488	Moriah	1,234	4,047
Liberty	1,359	4,460	Wildcat "E"	1,232	4,041

Mountain	Elev., m.	Elev., ft.	Mountain	Elev., m.	Elev., ft.
South Carter	1,359	4,458	Owl's Head	1,226	4,023
Hancock	1,342	4,403	Waumbek	1,225	4,020
Wildcat	1,340	4,397	Whiteface	1,224	4,015
South Kinsman	1,330	4,363	Isolation	1,221	4,005
Flume	1,319	4,327	Tecumseh	1,220	4,004
Field	1,319	4,326			

MAINE

Mountain	Elev., m.	Elev., ft.	Mountain	Elev., m.	Elev., ft.
Katahdin,			North Brother	1,263	4,143
Baxter Peak	1,605	5,267	Saddleback	1,255	4,116
Hamlin Peak	1,448	4,751	Bigelow,		
			Avery Peak	1,246	4,088
Sugarloaf	1,291	4,237	Abraham	1,234	4,049
Old Speck	1,274	4,180	The Horn,		
Crocker	1,270	4,168	Saddleback	1,226	4,023
Bigelow, W. Peak	1,265	4,150	Crocker, S. Peak	1,219	4,000

BOOKS ON HIKING, CLIMBING AND SKIING WESTERN UNITED STATES

Brower, David, ed.; *Manual of Ski Mountaineering;* Sierra Club, San Francisco, Calif.; 1962

Ferber, Peggy, ed.; *Mountaineering: The Freedom of the Hills;* The Mountaineers, Seattle, Wash.; 1974

LaChapelle, Edward R.; *The ABC of Avalanche Safety;* Colorado Outdoor Sports Co., Denver, Colo.; 1970

Prater, Gene; *Snowshoeing;* The Mountaineers, Seattle, Wash.; 1974

Tejada-Flores, Lito; *Backcountry Skiing: The Sierra Club Guide to Skiing Off the Beaten Track;* Sierra Club, San Francisco, Calif.; 1981

BOOKS AND ARTICLES ON NATURAL HISTORY AND ECOLOGY

Bentley, W. A. and Humphreys, W. J.; *Snow Crystals;* Dover Publications, N.Y.; 1931

Billings, William Dwight; "Plants in High Places"; *Natural History* (American Museum of Natural History); October, 1981

Blake, H. G. O., ed.; *Winter—From the Journal of Henry Thoreau;* Corner House Publishers, Williamstown, Mass.; 1973
Bliss, Lawrence C.; *Alpine Zone of the Presidential Range;* 1963
Carey, Cynthia and Marsh, Richard L.; "Shivering Finches"; *Natural History* (American Museum of Natural History); October, 1981
Couchman, J. K. et al; *Snow and Ice;* 1971
Fried, Marc B.; *Tales from the Shawangunk Mountains;* Adirondack Mountain Club, Glens Falls, N.Y.; 1981
Griffiths, John F.; *Applied Climatology;* Oxford University Press, N.Y.; 1966
Headstrom, Birger Richard; *Whose Track Is It?;* Ives Washburn, N.Y.; 1971
Hendrey, George R.; "Acid Rain and Gray Snow"; *Natural History* (American Museum of Natural History); February, 1981
Irving, Lawrence; "Adaptations to Cold"; *Scientific American*, Vol. 214, #1; January, 1966
Ketchledge, E. H.; *Trees of the Adirondack High Peak Region;* Adirondack Mountain Club, Glens Falls, N.Y.; 1979
Kirk, Ruth; *Snow;* Morrow Quill Paperbacks, N.Y.; 1977
Knutson, Roger M.; "Flowers that Make Heat while the Sun Shines"; *Natural History* (American Museum of Natural History); October, 1981
LaChapelle, Edward R.; *A Field Guide to Snow Crystals;* University of Washington Press, Seattle, Wash.; 1969
Morgan, Ann H.; *Field Book of Animals in Winter;* G. P. Putnam's Sons, N.Y.; 1939
Murie, Olaus; *A Field Guide to Animal Tracks;* Houghton Mifflin, Boston, Mass.; 1980
Pruitt, William; "Some Ecological Aspects of Snow"; *Proceedings, 1966; Helsinki Symposium on "Ecology of the Subarctic Regions"* — Paris, 1970; Department of Zoology, University of Manitoba
Pruitt, William; "Animals in the Snow"; *Scientific American;* January, 1960
Pruitt, William; "Life in the Snow"; *Manitoba Nature;* Winter 1973, Vol. 14, Issue 4
Rogers, Lynn; "A Bear in Its Lair"; *Natural History* (American Museum of Natural History); October, 1981
Russell, Helen Ross; *Winter Search Party—A Guide to Insects and other Invertebrates;* Thomas Nelson, Inc., Nashville, Tenn.; 1971

Serraro, John; "Insects and Spiders — How They Spend the Winter"; *The Conservationist;* November–December, 1976

Stokes, Donald W.; *A Guide to Nature in Winter;* Little, Brown & Co., Boston, Mass.; 1976

Taylor, Alexander R. and Fichter, George S.; *Ecology;* Golden Press, New York; 1973

Teale, E. W.; *Wandering through Winter;* Dodd Mead & Co., New York; 1973

Trelease, William; *Winter Botany;* Dover Publications, New York; 1967

Watts, Mary; *Winter Tree Finder;* Nature Study Guild, Berkeley, Calif.; 1970

Webster, David; *Snow Stumpers;* The Natural History Press, Garden City, New York; 1968

Wilson, Carl and Loomis, Walter; *Botany;* Holt, Rinehart & Winston, Chicago and New York; 1967

Wyckoff, Jerome; *The Adirondack Landscape;* Adirondack Mountain Club, Glens Falls, N.Y.; 1979

Zero, Edward J. and Mertz, Gregory; "Winter Wild Flowers"; *The Conservationist;* January–February, 1980

BIBLIOGRAPHY AND REFERENCES

1. Adams, Arthur G. et al; *Guide to the Catskills* — with Trail Guide and Maps; Walking News, N.Y.; 1975
2. Adirondack Mountain Club, Glens Falls, N.Y.: *Guide to Adirondack Trails — High Peak Region,* 1980; *Guide to the Northville-Placid Trail,* 1980; *Northern Adirondack Ski Tours* (Goodwin), 1982; *An Adirondack Sampler* (Wadsworth), 1979; *An Adirondack Sampler II* (Wadsworth), 1981
3. Appalachian Mountain Club, Boston, Mass.: *Maine Mountain Guide, 1976; White Mountain Guide,* 1979; *Massachusetts and Rhode Island Guide,* 1978; *Guide to Mount Washington and the Presidential Range,* 1976
4. Appalachian Trail Conference: Trail guides — *Maine,* 1978; *Massachusetts-Connecticut,* 1978; *New Hampshire-Vermont,* 1979; *New York-New Jersey,* 1977
5. Association of American Battery Manufacturers, Inc.
6. Astrand, Per-Olof and Rodahl, Kaare; *Textbook of Work Physiology;* McGraw-Hill; 1970

7. *Backpacker Magazine*, Kemsley, William Jr., ed. of: *Backpacking Equipment: A Consumer's Guide;* Macmillan Publishing Co., Inc., New York; 1978
8. Beiser, Karl; *25 Ski Tours in Maine;* New Hampshire Publishing Co., Somersworth, N.H.; 1979
9. Belding, Harwood W.; "Physiological Principles of Protection of Man in the Cold"; *Proceedings of a Conference, Quartermaster Research and Engineering Center,* Natick, Mass.; 1960; Man Living in the Arctic
10. Borg, A. and Veghte, J. H., ed.; "The Physiology of Cold Weather Survival"—*AGARD Report No. 620;* North Atlantic Treaty Organization; 1974
11. Boy Scouts of America; *Fieldbook for Boys and Men;* New Brunswick, N.J.; 1980
12. Brady, Michael and Skjemstad, Lorns; *Waxing for Cross-Country Skiing;* Wilderness Press, Berkeley, Calif.; 1977
13. Brady, Michael; *Cross-Country Ski Gear;* The Mountaineers, Seattle, Wash.; 1979
14. Brower, David, ed.; *Manual of Ski Mountaineering;* Sierra Club, San Francisco, Calif.; 1962
15. Caldwell, John; *Cross-Country Skiing Today;* The Steven Greene Press, Brattleboro, Vt.; 1977
16. Cary, Bob; *Winter Camping;* The Stephen Greene Press, Vt.; 1979
17. Coggeshall, Almy; *25 Ski Tours in the Adirondacks;* New Hampshire Publishing Co., Somersworth, N.H.; 1979
18. Connecticut Forest and Park Association; *Connecticut Walk Book;* Hartford, Conn.; 1975
19. Cunningham, Gerry and Hansson, Meg; *Lightweight Camping Equipment and How to Make It:* Ward, Colo.; 1976
20. Damon, Roger H., Jr.; "White Mountain Avalanche Hazard"; *Appalachia;* December, 1970
21. Danielsen, John A.; "How to Get Started in Winter Backpacking"; *Backpacker;* February, 1976
22. Darville, Fred T., Jr., M.D.; *Mountaineering Medicine;* Skagit Mountain Rescue Unit, Inc.; 1966
23. Department of Environmental Conservation, State of New York, Albany; *Nordic Skiing Trails in New York State;* 1977
24. Eastman Kodak Company; *Photography under Arctic Conditions*—*Pamphlet No. C-9;* Rochester, N.Y.; 1973

25. Fletcher, Colin; *The New Complete Walker;* Alfred A. Knopf, Inc., New York; 1974
26. Ford, Sally and Daniel; *25 Ski Tours in the White Mountains;* New Hampshire Publishing Co., Somersworth, N.H.; 1977
27. Frado, John; Lawson, Richard; and Coy, Robert; *25 Ski Tours in Western Massachusetts;* New Hampshire Publishing Co., Somersworth, N.H.; 1978
28. Gatty, Harold; *Nature Is Your Guide;* Penguin Books, New York; 1979
29. Goetze, Christopher; "Wind-Chill Factors"; *Appalachia;* December, 1975
30. Green Mountain Club, Rutland, Vt.: *Guidebook to the Long Trail,* 1979; *Day Hiker's Guide to Vermont,* 1978
31. Griswold, Lester; *Handicraft;* Lester Griswold, Colorado Springs, Colo.; 1937
32. Griswold, Whit; *Berkshire Trails for Walking and Ski Touring;* The East Woods Press, N.C.; 1979
33. Hammel, H. T.; "The Cold Climate Man"; *Proceedings of a Conference, Quartermaster Research and Engineering Center, Natick, Mass;* 1960; *Man Living in the Arctic*
34. Hedblom, E. E., Capt., M.C., U.S. Navy; *Polar Manual;* National Naval Medical Center, Bethesda, Md.; 1965
35. Henschel, Austin; "Arctic Rations"; *Proceedings of a Conference, Quartermaster Research and Engineering Center, Natick, Mass.;* 1960; *Man Living in the Arctic*
36. Innes-Taylor, Alan, ed.; *Arctic Survival Guide;* Scandinavian Airlines System, New York; 1957
37. Jaeger, Ellsworth; *Wildwood Wisdom;* The Macmillan Company, New York; 1953
38. Kjellstrom, Bjorn; *Be Expert with Map and Compass (The Orienteering Handbook);* Charles Scribner's Sons, New York; 1976
39. Knopp, Timothy B. and Maloney, Jack P.; *Ski Touring Planner;* The North Star Ski Touring Club of Minnesota and the U.S. Ski Association, Central Division; 1973
40. Kohler, Joseph and Wagner, Robert; "How Research Proves Stoves More Deadly Than Expected"; *Backpacker;* June, 1976
41. Lamoreaux, Marcia and Robert; *Outdoor Gear You Can Make Yourself;* Stackpole Books, Harrisburg, Penna.; 1976

42. Lathrop, Theodore G., M.D.; *Hypothermia: Killer of the Unprepared;* Mazamas, Portland, Ore.; 1970
43. Lederer, William T. and Wilson, Joe Pete; *Complete Cross-Country Skiing and Ski Touring;* W. W. Norton & Company, Inc., N.Y.; 1975
44. Lehr, Paul E. (et al); *Weather: A Guide to Phenomena and Forecasts;* Golden Press, N.Y.; 1975
45. Lorentzen, F. Vogt; *Cold: Physiology, Protection and Survival; AGARDOGRAPH No. 194, North Atlantic Treaty Organization;* 1973
46. Meehan, J. P.; "Protection of the Hands in Cold Weather"; *Summit Magazine;* November, 1960
47. Mills, William J., Jr.; "Frostbite—A Discussion of the Problem and a Review of an Alaskan Experience"; *Alaska Medicine;* March, 1973
48. Muench, Stuart; "Radio Weather Information in the White Mountains"; *Appalachia;* December, 1973
49. National Weather Service (U.S. Government); *Winter Storms;* 1974
50. Newburgh, L. H., ed.; *Physiology of Heat Regulation and the Science of Clothing;* W. B. Saunders, Philadelphia; 1949
51. Osgood, William E. and Hurley, Leslie, Jr.; *The Snowshoe Book;* Stephen Greene Press, Brattleboro, Vt.; 1975
52. Prater, Gene; *Snowshoeing;* The Mountaineers, Seattle, Wash.; 1980
53. Prater, Yvonne and Mendenhall, Ruth Dyer; *Gorp, Glop & Glue Stew;* The Mountaineers, Seattle, Wash.; 1982
54. Pruitt, William O., Jr.; "Life in the Snow"; *Manitoba Nature;* Winter, 1973
55. Putnam, William; *Snow Conditions;* Appalachian Mountain Club, Boston, Mass.; 1961
56. Rethmel, R. C.; *Backpacking;* Follett Publishing Company, Chicago, Ill.; 1979
57. Rutstrum, Calvin; *The Wilderness Route Finder;* The Macmillan Company, N.Y.; 1974
58. Siple, Paul A.; *90°South;* G. P. Putnam's Sons, N.Y.; 1959
59. Ski Touring Council, Inc.; *Ski Touring Guide;* Ski Touring Council, Inc.; 1978
60. Smutek, Raymond; "Lightweight Stoves for Mountaineering"; *Off Belay,* Renton, Wash.; 1975
61. Sumner, Robert; *Make Your Own Camping Equipment;* Drake Publisher, Inc., N.Y.; 1976

BIBLIOGRAPHY AND REFERENCES

62. Tapley, Lance; *Ski Touring in New England;* Stone Wall Press, Lexington, Mass.; 1976
63. Union Carbide Corporation, General Electric Company and Power Conversion, Inc.
64. Waddell, Gordon; "Energy Requirements of Mountain Walking"; *Summit Magazine;* March, 1966
65. Washburn, Bradford; *Frostbite—What It Is; How to Prevent It; Emergency Treatment;* Museum of Science, Boston, Mass.; 1972
66. Wass, Stan, with Alvord, David W.; *25 Ski Tours in Connecticut;* New Hampshire Publishing Co., Somersworth, N.H.; 1978
67. Wilder, Edna; *Secrets of Eskimo Skin Sewing;* Alaska Northwest Publishing Co., Anchorage, Alaska; 1976
68. Wilkerson, James A., M.D. (ed.); *Medicine for Mountaineering;* The Mountaineers, Seattle, Wash.; 1976
69. Ziegler, Katey, (ed.); *Ski Touring Guide to New England;* Eastern Mountain Sports, Peterborough, N.H.; 1979

Index

Abuses, trail, 200
Acclimatization, 1
Adirondack Mountains:
  Elevations, 208
  Weather, 192
Altimeters, 97
Anorak, 28
Anoxis, 24
Asphyxiation hazards, 23, 169
Avalanche hazards, 141
Awareness, environmental, 200

Batteries, 99
  Lithium, 101
  Rechargeable, 101
  Temperature effects, 99
Battery booster cables, 145
Beard, inconvenience of, 22
Beverages, 114
Bindings:
  Ski, 75
  Snowshoe, 67
Bleeding, treatment for, 25
Body:
  Effects of cold, 1
  Signals, 174
  Temperature variations, 13
Books and articles:
  Bibliography, 212
  Natural history and ecology, 210
  Western U.S., 210
Boots (see also ski boots)
  Frostbite and, 22
  Keeping feet dry, 38, 42, 44
  Keeping snow out, 38
  Table of, 42
Braking:
  On skis, 132
  On snowshoes, 119
Breathing, cooling by, 12

Cameras and film, 102
Camping:
  Procedures, 150
  Tents, 83
Candle:
  As warning device, 24
  Heat from, 176
Carbon dioxide, 23

Carbon monoxide, 23
Car use, 144
Casualty reports, 182
Catskills:
  Elevations, 208
Cave, snow, 170
Chains, for car, 146
Chocolate, effects of, 23
Circulation:
  Affected by chilling, 13, 16
  Body heat and, 11
  Frostbite and, 16
  Shock and, 20
Climbers—see ski climbers
Clothing, 27
  Basic requirements, 27
  Bodywear, 32
  Boots, 38
  Checking before hike, 5
  Checklist, 46
  Cotton, 27
  Frostbite and, 18, 22
  Gloves and mittens, 35
  Headgear, 46
  Inactive person, 30
  New fabrics, 34
  Pants, 34
  Shirts, 32
  Socks, 42, 44
  Underwear, 30
  Ventilation, 27, 29
Cloud formation, 186
Coffee, effects of, 23
Cold:
  Adaptation to, 1
  Injured person, effect on, 25
Cold objects, handling, 20
Compasses, 95
Conduction, heat loss by, 11
Constipation, effects of, 22
Convection, heat loss by, 11
Cooking, 111, 152
Cotton, 27
Crampons, 59
Creepers, 45
Cross-country skiing—see ski touring
Crossing ice, 139

Dead reckoning, 162
Dehydrated foods, 112
Dehydration, 23, 114
Dinner, preparing, 111, 152
Down, 27, 53

Emergencies: (see also survival and rescue)
  Equipment checklist, 177
  First aid, 15, 21, 25
  Food for, 176
  Heat sources for, 175
  Shelter for, 169
  Signaling, 172
Energy expenditure, 110
Environment:
  Awareness, 200
  Hiker's personal code, 203
  Mountain summits, impact on, 200
  Trail abuses, 200
Equipment (see also specific items)
  Basic, 5
  Checking before hike, 5
  Checklist, 105
Evaporation:
  Cooling by, 11
  Dehydration by, 11, 23
Exhaustion—see fatigue
Exposure—see hypothermia

Face mask, 8, 22, 46
Fatigue, 14, 20, 22
Film, camera, 104
Fire making, 174
First aid, 25
Fishnet underwear, 30
Flashlights, 99
Food, 109
  Beverages, 114
  Checklist, 114
  Dehydrated, 112
  Energy from, 111
  Environmental cost, 112
  Extended trip, 111
  Freeze-dried, 112
  Lack of, 10
  One-day trip, 110
  One-pot meal, 111
  Requirements, 109
  Salt intake, 114
  Survival, 176
  Utensils, 111
  Vitamins, 113
Fractures, splinting for, 26
Framepack, 29, 49
Frostbite, 16
  Causes, 18
  First aid, 21
  Nature of, 16
  Preventing, 22
  Symptoms, 17
  Tourniquet may cause, 25
Frostnip, 17, 21

Gaiters, 38, 78
Gasoline:
  Cooling by, 20
  For Stoves, 90
Glaze, 189
Gloves, 35
  Inserts, 37
  Objects handled with, 20, 37
Green Mountains:
  Elevations, 209
Ground signals, 175

Handling cold objects, 20, 37
Hands, rewarming, 37
Headgear, 46
Headlights, 99
Heat:
  Emergency, 175
  Loss of, 11
  Production and conservation, 11
High peaks of Northeast, 208
Hiker's personal code, 203
Hypothermia, 13
  Emergency treatment, 15
  Events causing, 14
  Incidence, 16
  Symptoms, 15

Ice:
  Axes, 61
  Crossing, 139
  Rescue, 140
Inactive person, clothing for, 30
Injuries—see first aid

Jacket, 29, 33

Leadership and leaders, 3
Littering, 112, 203

Magnetic bearings, 160
Maine:
   Mountain elevations, 210
Maps and compasses, 95
Metric equivalents, 206
Microclimate, 190
Mirror, signaling, 173
Mittens, 35
Moon, finding directions by, 168
Mountains of Northeast, 208
Mukluks, canvas, 40

Natural history and ecology, 210
Navigation, cross-country, 158
Nose, running, 13

One-pot meal, 111
Organization, need for, 3
Orienteering, 96
Orion, directions from, 168
Overheating, 22
Oxygen deficiency, 10, 23

Pacing a hike, 6
Packboard, 52
Packs and framepacks, 29, 49
Pads and air mattresses, 59
Pants, 34
   Snowproofing, 38
Parka, 32
Perspiration:
   Cooling by, 11
   Ventilation, 27, 29
Polaris (pole star), 166
Position finding, 162
Precipitation, 188, 192, 197
Preparation, importance of, 1, 186
Pulks, 97

Radiation, heat loss by, 11
Radio weather reports, 197
Rain, formation of, 188
Rescue, 177

Salt intake, 114
Shelter, 150
Shirts, 32
Shivering, 11
Shock, 20, 25
Shovels, snow, 106
Signals, emergency, 172

Ski:
   Boots and bindings, 75
   Checking binding, 79
   Choosing skis, 82
   Climbers, 130
   Failures, 135
   Improving control, 82
   Poles, 74
   Preventing injury, 79, 82
   Repairs, 135
Ski touring:
   Conditions, Northeast, 120
   Orienteering, 96
   Trail design, 123
   Where to go, 147
Sleds, 97
   Emergency, 179
   Folding, 98
Sleeping, 153
   Precautions, 23
Sleeping bags, 52
   Cleaning of, 57
Sleet, 189
Smoking, effects of, 21
Snow:
   Formation of, 188
   Shelters, 153, 169
   Travel affected by, 1, 117
Snowboat (pulk), 97
Snowhouse, 153
Snow-mound house, 156
Snow shelters, 153
   Warmth from, 190
Snowshoeing, 117
Snowshoes, 62
   Bindings, 67
   Crampons, 66
   Guide, 68
   Poles, 70
Snow tires, 146
Socks, 42
   Changing, 44
   Frostbite and, 21
Splints, 26
Stars, directions from, 163
Stoves, 88
   Carbon monoxide from, 23
   Heat in fuels, 95
   Table of, 93
Sun, finding directions from, 165

220 INDEX

Survival and rescue:
  Food, emergency, 176
  Heat, emergency, 175
  Rescue, 177
  Shelter, emergency, 168
  Shelters, relative warmth of, 192
  Signals, emergency, 173
Suspenders, 29
Sweaters, 32
Synthetic fabrics:
  Nylon pile, 28
  Breathable, 34

Tea, effects of, 23
Temperature equivalents, 207
Tents, 83
  Breaking camp, 153
  Cooking in, 111, 152
  Features of a winter tent, 85
  Placing and securing, 150
  Sleeping in, 153
  Table of, 86
  Types, 84
Terrain features, 205
Thermal-knit underwear, 32
Thirst—see dehydration
Topographical maps, 95
Tourniquet, 25
Travel, 117
  Emergency ski binding, 136
  Pole braking, 132
  Ski climbers, 130
  Ski climbing methods, 130
  Ski touring and mountaineering, 120
  Ski waxing guide, 127, 129
  Snowshoeing, 116
Trench shelter, 171

Undershirts, string, 30
Underwear, 30
Utensils for eating, 111

Ventilation:
  Clothing, 27, 29
  Snow shelter, 170
  Tents, 23
Vest, 34
Vitamins, 113

Water:
  Body's need for, 23, 114
  Snow as source, 111, 114
Waxes, ski, 123
Weather:
  Adirondacks-White Mountains, 192
  Beaufort scale, 191
  Forecast by leader, 5
  Microclimate, 190
  Northeastern, 196
  Precipitation, 188, 194
  Preparation for worst, 186
  Radio reports, 197
  Winter storms, 198
Western U.S., books, 210
Wetting:
  Hazards of, 14, 20, 57
  Insulation affected, 29
Where to go, 147
White Mountains:
  Elevations, 209
  Weather, 192
Wind, 190, 192
  Beaufort scale, 191
  Directions indicated by, 163
  Protection from, 22, 28, 32
Windchill, 11, 18, 190
Wind pants, 34
Winter conditions, travel affected by, 1
Winter schools, 6
Wood fire, 174
Wool, 27

Other Publications
of
The Adirondack Mountain Club, Inc.
172 Ridge Street
Glens Falls, N.Y. 12801
(518) 793-7737

Guidebooks

GUIDE TO ADIRONDACK TRAILS—High Peak Region
Definitive guide to the High Peaks
GUIDE TO THE NORTHVILLE-PLACID TRAIL
Detailed description and guide to 133-mile trail
GUIDE TO THE EASTERN ADIRONDACKS
Lake George, Pharaoh Lake, and Beyond
GUIDE TO TRAILS OF THE WEST-CENTRAL ADIRONDACKS
Hiking trails and canoe route from Old Forge area to Blue Mountain Lake
OLD ROADS AND OPEN PEAKS
Walks, climbs, canoe routes, bushwhacks in Great Sacandaga Lake-Johnsburg area
ADIRONDACK CANOE WATERS—NORTH FLOW
Definitive guide to over 700 miles of canoe routes in St. Lawrence/Lake Champlain drainage basins
AN ADIRONDACK SAMPLER, Day Hikes for All Seasons
50 hikes throughout the Adirondack Park; includes winter hikes for the snowshoer
AN ADIRONDACK SAMPLER II, Backpacking Trips
25 trips throughout the Park for novice and expert
NORTHERN ADIRONDACK SKI TOURS
30 selected tours for the novice to expert skier

Natural History

THE ADIRONDACK LANDSCAPE
Complete hiker's guide to common High Peak land forms
TREES OF THE ADIRONDACK HIGH PEAK REGION
Hiker's identification guide to trees in the Forest Preserve
ROCK SCENERY OF THE HUDSON HIGHLANDS AND PALISADES
Guide to the geology of southern New York State
BIRDLIFE OF THE ADIRONDACK PARK
Complete text for researcher, describing 261 species accounts

General Reading

PEAKS AND PEOPLE OF THE ADIRONDACKS
Geography and lore of the Adirondack High Peaks
TALES FROM THE SHAWANGUNK MOUNTAINS
A naturalist's musings, a bushwhacker's guide

Maps

Trails of the Adirondack High Peak Region
 USGS quads of Marcy, Santanoni, half of Elizabethtown
Old Roads and Open Peaks of the Sacandaga Region
 Portions of USGS quads of Indian Lake, 13th Lake, North Creek, Lake Pleasant, Harrisburg, Lake Luzerne
Trails of the West-Central Adirondacks
 Old Forge area to Blue Mountain Lake

Price List available on request